RISK MANAGEMENT AND INSURANCE MANUAL
FOR LIBRARIES

RISK MANAGEMENT AND INSURANCE MANUAL FOR LIBRARIES
UPDATED

SALLY ALEXANDER
MARY BREIGHNER

EDITED BY
JEANNE M. DREWES

IN COLLABORATION WITH CORE PUBLISHING

ALA
Editions
CHICAGO 2021

© 2021 by the American Library Association

Extensive effort has gone into ensuring the reliability of the information in this book; however, the publisher makes no warranty, express or implied, with respect to the material contained herein.

ISBN: 978-0-8389-4801-9

Library of Congress Cataloging-in-Publication Data

Names: Alexander, Sally, 1970- author. | Breighner, Mary, author. | Drewes, Jeanne M., editor. | Breighner, Mary. Risk and insurance management manual for libraries.
Title: Risk management and insurance manual for libraries / Sally Alexander, Mary Breighner ; edited by Jeanne M. Drewes.
Description: Updated. | Chicago : ALA Editions in collaboration with ALCTS Publishing, 2021. | Series: An ALCTS monograph | This new version updates and expands the previous edition to cover many new issues affecting libraries including cyber security and cyber-attacks and incorporates broader principles of risk management including enterprise risk management concepts. | Includes bibliographical references and index. | Summary: "This manual offers plain language guidance for trustees and administrators for designing and implementing a library risk management program"— Provided by publisher.
Identifiers: LCCN 2020019113 | ISBN 9780838948019 (paperback)
Subjects: LCSH: Libraries—Risk management—Handbooks, manuals, etc. | Libraries—Insurance—Handbooks, manuals, etc.
Classification: LCC Z683.5 .A44 2020 | DDC 025.1—dc23
LC record available at https://lccn.loc.gov/2020019113

Cover design by Kim Thornton.

♾ This paper meets the requirements of ANSI/NISO Z39.48-1992 (Permanence of Paper).

Printed in the United States of America
25 24 23 22 21   5 4 3 2 1

Disclaimer

This manual is intended to serve as a reference guide on various aspects of risk management and insurance, including bringing to the attention of the user potential hazards or conditions related to the existence and operation of libraries. The user must make the decision on whether and how to address any hazard or condition. Any resources listed in the text or the appendixes do not constitute an endorsement by the authors or editors. No liability is assumed by or through the use of any information contained in the manual.

Contents

Preface

This book is an updated version of the 2005 edition of the *Risk and Insurance Management Manual for Libraries*. It broadens the previous manual and incorporates broader principles of risk management, including enterprise risk management concepts. The current authors are indebted to William Payton for the previous version of the text. We are also grateful to Jeanne Drewes for her guidance and contributions to the text, especially those sections relating directly to library valuations.

EDITOR'S NOTE

This new edition updates and expands the previous edition to cover the many new issues affecting libraries, including cybersecurity and cyberattacks. Additional appendixes are also included and additional hazards, such as earthquakes, are discussed. The world feels like a more dangerous place nowadays, and the current authors have tried to consider all possible issues that may affect libraries. Risk management and insurance industry terminology is used throughout in the hope that this will assist the library community both in their communications with their insurance agent and consultants as well as in better understanding the terms within insurance policies and contracts. I am particularly grateful to Mary Breighner for continuing to share her deep expertise and for suggesting (as coauthor) the incomparable Sally Alexander, who provided additional invaluable expertise for this edition. These two authors spent countless hours editing and adding more current information to make this edition far more useful for 2020. It takes experts willing to dedicate their time and share their expertise without remuneration to produce a publication of such high quality. The staff at the ALA and the ALCTS monograph editorial board are also to be recognized for their work in encouraging the completion of this book.

In March 2020, the Association for Library Collections & Technical Services (ALCTS), Library and Information Technology Association (LITA), and Library Leadership & Management Association (LLAMA) voted to jointly form Core: Leadership, Infrastructure, Futures, a division of the American Library Association. Core cultivates and celebrates the collective expertise of library workers in core functions through community building, advocacy, and learning. Core will formally launch September 2020.

It is appropriate that this is the first publication since the creation of Core, which unites the sections that worked together on earlier versions of this manual. I am particularly pleased after being part of both the Preservation & Reformatting Section (PARS) and LLAMA in this area of risk management and insurance, now working under the umbrella of Core (core.ala.org). This manual provides a current reference for public, academic, and special libraries concerning issues of risk management and insurance.

Jeanne Drewes, Editor

Introduction

Risk management and insurance are closely related, each impacting the other. Lowering risk can reduce the cost of insurance, and insurance can cover many of the unexpected hazards that a risk review cannot eliminate. The authors have worked to consider as many risks as possible and to provide meaningful options for reducing them, while acknowledging that there will always be risks and hazards in any public building that provides resources to a varied community of users and visitors. The concept of a manual has been retained in this book. This is not a textbook; rather, it covers a broad spectrum of issues and actions, while also providing some resources for further investigation. We have tried to avoid too much depth of detail, while assisting those responsible for designing, implementing, and administering a library risk management program. The participants of a risk management team should include trustees, directors, and librarians as well as facilities, safety, and security personnel, and may also include underwriters, consultants, agents, and brokers. We hope that the examples and guidance in this book provide library personnel with an effective risk management and insurance program for development. While this book predominantly focuses on property and casualty insurance, additional hazards and insurance options have been discussed to better enable the reader to select from the consideration of the options for reducing risk. This manual is intended for United States libraries, and while foreign librarians may find useful information, government regulations and laws of their particular country should be considered before adopting the information provided here.

OBJECTIVES

This manual's objectives are the same as the earlier edition:

1. To inform trustees, directors, librarians, and other library personnel of the essential elements and concepts of an appropriate risk management and insurance program for libraries.
2. To assist those who are responsible for designing, implementing, and administering a library risk management program, including all members of the risk management team. The team's participants should include trustees, directors, librarians, and safety and security personnel, and may also include underwriters, consultants, agents, and brokers.
3. To provide a guide for library personnel so an effective risk management and insurance program can be developed.

A discussion of group insurance for employees has been purposely omitted from this manual. The subject material of this manual is limited to property and casualty risk management and insurance. Employee benefits, such as medical and disability insurance, are not included because the insurance needs of employees are not unique to libraries and frequently are provided through coverage by a library's parent organization.

1

A Risk Management Philosophy for Libraries

RESPONSIBILITY OF THE LIBRARY BOARD OF DIRECTORS OR TRUSTEES

Whether the library is part of an institution or other organization or is a separate legal entity, the ultimate authority for its operation lies with a board of directors, trustees, or other governing body. The obligations and responsibilities of this board may be defined by state statute, or the board may, to a large extent, be subject to common law rules. In any event, there are both a moral and a legal obligation calling for the exercise of good business judgment in protecting the library's assets, and its reputation. This requires the directors and trustees to identify all risks of loss to which the library may be exposed as a result of its operations. Having identified the risks of loss, the directors have the ultimate responsibility to deal with those risks to minimize the adverse financial consequences of losses that may result from those risks. In short, the board is responsible for the development of an enterprise risk management policy for the library.

The directors and trustees have an obligation to identify risks and take steps to minimize the risk of loss to either the library or another person or entity. The board's risk oversight role should include their proposed strategy and risk appetite, as well as the alignment of that strategy and operational objectives with the library's mission and values. The board can, however, delegate the implementation of the enterprise risk management policy to others, including the administrator, business officer, controller, treasurer, librarian, or other person. In most cases, this is what is done. Even when the library is part of a municipality, university, or larger organization, the library administrator, the controller, and the library administrator must be provided with standards or guidelines. These standards or guidelines should delegate authority to identify and manage risks, including the purchasing of insurance. A risk management policy statement should be developed by the board and disseminated throughout the library to those responsible for carrying out the business policies of the board.

WHAT IS RISK?

One cannot implement an appropriate enterprise risk management framework without defining what we mean by risk. The word risk has many definitions:

- "the effect of uncertainty on objectives" (ISO 2018).
- "combination of the likelihood and the consequence(s) of a specified hazardous event occurring" (OHSAS 1999, 3).
- ISO 31000:2009 and ISO Guide 73 changes risk to the "effect of uncertainty on objectives" (Wikipedia 2020). This means that the definition has been expanded to refer to positive and negative consequences of uncertainty.

In short, risk is the occurrence of any event which is uncertain, and which when it does occur will have a consequence or an impact. The consequence can either be negative—such as causing financial loss, or it can be positive—such as providing an opportunity for an organization.

WHAT IS RISK MANAGEMENT?

The term risk management has a variety of definitions:

- "Risk management is the identification, measurement and treatment of property, liability, and personnel pure-risk exposures" (Williams and Heins 1985, 16).
- Risk management "is concerned with the systematic organized effort to eliminate or reduce harm to persons and the threat of losses to public organizations" (Reed and Swain 1990, 261).

- "Risk management can be defined as a systematic process for the identification and evaluation of pure loss exposures faced by an organization or individual, and for the selection and administration of the most appropriate techniques for treating such exposures" (Rejda 1992, 47).
- "Risk management is a broad-based, systematic approach to preventing accidental losses, reducing the cost of losses that occur, and finding the most efficient way to pay for whatever losses remain" (Trupin and Flitner 1998, 2).
- "The Alliance for Nonprofit Management defines risk management as, '[...] a discipline for dealing with the possibility that some future event will cause harm. It provides strategies, techniques, and an approach to recognizing and confronting any threat faced by an organization in fulfilling its mission'" (Layne 2019).

WHAT IS ENTERPRISE RISK MANAGEMENT?

Like risk management, the term enterprise risk management has a number of definitions.

- "Enterprise risk management is a process, effected by an entity's board of directors, management, and other personnel, applied in strategy setting and across the enterprise, [that is] designed to identify potential events that may affect the entity, and manage risk to be within its risk appetite, to provide reasonable assurance regarding the achievement of entity objectives" (COSO 2004).
- "Enterprise risk management is a plan-based business strategy that aims to identify, assess, and prepare for any dangers, hazards, and other potentials for disaster—both physical and figurative—that may interfere with an organization's operations and objectives" (Kenton 2019).

For a more detailed discussion about ERM, please see discussion at end of this chapter.

There is considerable similarity between the definitions of enterprise risk management and traditional risk management. Common to both is the recognition that risk management is a process that allows an organization to identify and manage its risk. No matter which definition the library prefers, risk management is a systematic process of identifying, analyzing, and quantifying the risks of human, physical, and financial loss to preserve the assets of the library by selecting the most appropriate method of managing those risks through avoidance, prevention, reduction, knowing assumption, transfer of the risk of loss to others, or by the purchase of insurance.

RISK MANAGEMENT AND INSURANCE

Insurance is an important part of the risk management program. It is a method that organizations use to finance their risk—that is, to protect the organization from the potential economic impact of losses or claims. Risk management is a broader concept than insurance. It places greater emphasis on the identification, analysis, prevention, and control of risks. Insurance is only one tool in the risk management process. Risk management recognizes that some risks can be avoided; that other risks can be reduced or eliminated; and that additional risks can be transferred to others. In this regard, some risks are insurable, some not; and some risks involve types of losses that should be insured against by the purchase of commercial insurance, while others are losses that can be assumed or self-insured. Issues of primary importance in risk management are loss prevention and loss control, insurance, and communication. When fully implemented, risk management decisions have a greater impact on library operations than insurance alone and can add value to the library by helping avoid or minimize major financial losses, and by making the library a safer place in which to learn and work. These principles are readily adaptable to libraries—large, small, public, private, university, or special.

THE RISK MANAGEMENT PROCESS

Risk management is a decision-making process. This process involves several steps—all designed to help reduce uncertainty concerning the occurrence of a future loss, or opportunity. The process consists of several steps: risk identification, risk quantification and evaluation, risk treatment implementation, and reevaluation.

RISK IDENTIFICATION

The first step in the risk management process is to identify risks to which the library may be subject. At the operational level, this will involve an analysis of the operations of the library and identification of the risks inherent in those operations. In this step, the library will identify those assets or operations that, if damaged or destroyed, would cause difficulty to ongoing operations.

These include the physical assets of the library, such as the building and its collections; the human assets, including all employees and volunteers, particularly those who are specially trained in skills critical to the library's functions; financial assets that might be subject to theft; and the risks present in the library's operations, such as trip-and-fall hazards. Simply put, in this step the library is looking to determine who could be at risk as a result of the library's operations and what could be damaged, destroyed, or lost as a result of the library's operations. Chapter 2, "Risk Identification," discusses this step of the risk management process in more detail.

The board should identify risks that the library may have at a strategic level and set the risk appetite for the library. This will be discussed in more detail later in this chapter.

RISK QUANTIFICATION AND EVALUATION

The next step in the process is to quantify the risks identified in step one. This involves an evaluation of the potential size of losses that may occur from the different risks identified, and evaluating the likelihood that such losses will occur. In other words, the library will evaluate the probable frequency and severity of losses from various risks.

For severity or impact, the library should consider not only financial impacts but impacts that relate to its mission. Mission impacts include reputational impacts.

For example, what is the likelihood of having property damaged or lost from any number of causes, such as fire, flood, or wind? And what is the estimated size of the damage that might ensue? For what operations, actions, and inactions might the library be held liable under law if any of those result in bodily injury to someone else or damage to someone else's property? Chapter 3, "Risk Quantification and Evaluation," discusses this step of the risk management process in more detail. Arguably, the first two steps in the risk management process are the most critical ones. The more accurate these assessments are, the more effective the program designed to manage the risks can be.

Once potential risks of loss have been identified and quantified, the library needs to evaluate and select the most effective risk treatment method to manage these risks. In evaluating the options, the library must balance the desire to reduce risk and prevent losses with an understanding that risks are an inherent part of any library operation. Therefore, while some risks can be managed without a disruption to operations, many cannot. These risks must be dealt with in a way that decreases the likelihood a loss may occur and that limits the impact to the library, yet allows the library to continue its mission of service to its constituents.

RISK TREATMENT STRATEGIES

Risk treatment strategies include risk avoidance. Avoidance can be the most effective risk management strategy, but for many risks inherent in the library's operations, it may not be practical or even possible in the context of the library's mission of service to its community. Yet, some risks can be avoided without causing disruption to library operations. It is advisable to manage risks wherever possible and feasible. For example, the library could prohibit the consumption of alcohol at special events held on its premises.

Other risk treatment strategies include loss prevention and control strategies, financing the risk through the purchase of insurance, and transferring the risk through the contractual transfer of risk.

LOSS PREVENTION AND CONTROL

Many risks of loss can be managed or significantly reduced by loss prevention activities. Some examples include training drivers to operate more safely in order to reduce the likelihood of auto accidents; training workers in proper lifting techniques to limit the potential for injuries; and installing smoke detectors, fire alarms, and automatic sprinkler systems to prevent or limit smoke and fire damage. These are actions that the library can take to reduce the likelihood of loss or minimize the losses that do occur for those risks the library accepts as part of doing business. Chapter 4, "Loss Prevention," discusses this step of the risk management process in more detail.

RISK FINANCING

Ultimately, many risks will remain both part of the library's operations and its financial responsibility. Therefore, risk financing is a major component of the risk management process. Risk financing is the process of selecting the most cost-effective means of ensuring that funds will be available after a loss to allow the library to rebuild and restore damaged or destroyed property and to continue its mission of service to its constituents. While the library can deal with the financial obligations incumbent with some operational risks, most libraries will not be able to, or desire to, be responsible for the adverse financial consequences of large losses. Risk financing involves three options: non-insurance transfer, self-insurance, and the purchase of commercial insurance. Risk financing is discussed in greater detail in chapter 5, "Risk Financing."

TRANSFERRING THE RISK TO OTHERS

Whenever possible, risks should be transferred from the library to others with whom it does business via a non-insurance transfer, such as "hold harmless" or indemnity clauses in contracts with third parties. An indemnity clause or hold harmless agreement written into a contract or lease agreement will provide that a third party contracting with the library will accept financial responsibility for losses caused by that third party's negligent operations on behalf of the library. Chapter 5 examines this concept in more detail.

SELF-INSURANCE

Self-insurance is defined as "the conscious retention of risk, the level of which has been limited within the financial capacity of the firm, emanating from a distribution of exposures that permit reasonable predictions as to future loss probabilities" (Goshay 1964, 21). "Self-insurance" is not the same as "no insurance" in that self-insurance involves a specific decision to absorb the financial consequences of a particular loss or type of loss, after the risk of loss has been identified and quantified. Responsible organizations that self-insure should set aside monies or earmark resources to fund identified self-insured losses. Chapter 5 discusses this concept in more detail.

PURCHASE INSURANCE

Commercial insurance is insurance coverage that is provided by an insurance company in exchange for a fixed payment that is agreed upon in advance. As a general guideline, commercial insurance should be purchased when the probability or likelihood of loss is low, but the potential severity or impact of any loss that may occur is high. Any risks to the library that involve significant physical damage to its buildings, facilities, collections, or equipment, or that involve large financial losses from some other cause, should be managed by the use of commercial insurance. Two other types of risks are also reasons for the purchase of commercial insurance:

- those for which the law requires insurance (such as bonds on specified library employees, workers' compensation)
- those in which the insurer may have expertise and provide valuable services that justify the purchase of insurance, even though the library has the financial capacity to absorb the losses that might be expected (such as boiler and machinery insurance)

Generally, libraries should at least consider purchasing the following types of insurance: workers' compensation; property, boiler, and machinery; general and excess liability; automobile liability; directors' and officers' liability; and cyber liability and fiduciary liability. Chapter 6, "Risk Financing—Insurance," is an extensive discussion of commercial insurance and its various types.

REEVALUATION

Finally, the library should reevaluate its risk management process on a periodic basis. Risk treatment strategies need to be evaluated to determine whether they are in fact managing the risk. Some risk treatment strategies may generate unforeseen consequences, and some risk treatment strategies may not be effective. In addition, it is important to reevaluate the risk management process to assure its alignment with the board's strategic goals, as well as the mission and values of the organization. This is especially important if the library has opened new facilities, launched new programs, or executed non-insurance transfers.

A RISK MANAGEMENT POLICY STATEMENT

Risk management is a process in which everyone in the library has a role to play. It is also an attitude that must be adopted by everyone in the library. That attitude, when adopted by all staff, leads to a safer environment for staff as well as for the library's customers. In addition, adopting a strong commitment to risk management will ensure that the library's physical assets are well protected and the likelihood of loss is decreased. Because the board has the primary responsibility for establishing the risk management philosophy, it also has primary responsibility for developing and promulgating a risk management policy statement for the library's staff that lays the foundation for the risk management attitude. But simply developing a policy is not enough. It is the board's responsibility to see that its risk management policy is effectively communicated throughout the library.

The library's risk management policy statement, first and foremost, should set forth the library's philosophy regarding risk management. It should state unequivocally the library's commitment to risk identification and examination and to proactive risk management. The policy statement should designate the individual or individuals who shall have the administrative responsibility for overseeing the policy in day-to-day operations. It should delegate operational risk and insurance management responsibility and authority to the administrator or some other person. The policy statement may provide the parameters of that authority, as well as delineate what areas will remain within the sole jurisdiction of the board, such as strategy setting and financial risk appetite.

The risk management policy statement should enumerate how the risk management principles adopted by the board will be applied. This policy should take into consideration the financial condition of the library, its access to additional funds for self-insured and uninsured losses, and its obligation to provide uninterrupted service to its constituents. The risk management policy statement may assign responsibility for determining the form of insurance coverage, the insurance policy's terms and conditions, the amount of coverage and limits of liability, and the amount of any deductible or self-insured retention. It may designate the types of services to be used (consultants, agents, or brokers), and it may prescribe requirements relating to the bidding of insurance coverage. A "Sample Risk Management and Insurance Policy" statement is contained in appendix B.

THE ADMINISTRATOR'S RESPONSIBILITY

The library and its risk management and insurance needs are unique in several ways. The library's most valuable assets are its collections. They have special valuation issues, and their services cannot be readily provided by the use of substitute facilities. In most cases, the administrator is the person who should be relied upon for much of the information essential to establishing a risk management and insurance program.

If the library is part of an institution that employs a professional risk manager (or other officer responsible for administering risk management), the administrator should be involved in various stages of the risk management process and work with the risk manager to identify and quantify fully the risks of loss to which the library is exposed. Only after fully knowing and assessing the risks can the library develop an adequate insurance program to properly protect itself in the event of loss. Once insurance coverage has been placed, the administrator should thoroughly understand the lines of coverage that apply to the library's operations and its building and contents, as well as the amount of deductibles the library may be called upon to absorb. The administrator should also understand the extent of recovery that can be expected in the event of a loss in relation to the cost of repairing the damage—in other words, how much financial strain, if any, may be placed upon the library's budget in the event of a probable loss.

Whether the library is a small, public library or part of a very large institution, a risk management policy statement is desirable as a guide for the librarian. This should embody the risk management concepts discussed throughout this manual, and it should contain parameters relating to risks to be assumed (self-insured), risks to be covered by commercial insurance, and deductibles to be accepted (refer to appendix B for a sample risk management policy).

ENTERPRISE RISK MANAGEMENT AND LIBRARIES

Whether a library is part of a larger organization such as part of a university or city or county, or is a separate entity, such as a public or private stand-alone library, enterprise risk management (ERM) may be a useful decision-making/ management framework that can be incorporated into the overall governance of the library.

The purpose of this chapter is to introduce the ERM concept and provide some context and advice should a library decide that it wants to pursue the ERM framework. ERM is a relatively new concept, and many organizations may have difficulty creating an ERM framework that is optimal and efficient, and that adds value. Our hope is that should you decide to pursue ERM, you can do so in a way that adds value to your organization. If your library is already part of an institution that is using the ERM framework, we hope that this chapter will allow for additional discussions.

WHAT IS ENTERPRISE RISK MANAGEMENT?

We cannot begin unless we have a clear understanding of what we mean by ERM. Like the definition for risk management, the term enterprise risk management has a number of definitions. It will be helpful to review these definitions again:

- "Enterprise risk management is a process, effected by an entity's board of directors, management or other personnel, applied in strategy setting and across the enterprise, designed to identify potential events that may affect the entity, and manage risks to be within its risk appetite, to provide reasonable assurance regarding the achievement of entity objectives" (COSO 2004).

In the COSO definition "entity" would mean "library."

- "Enterprise risk management is a plan-based business strategy that aims to identify, assess, and prepare for any dangers, hazards, and other potentials for disaster—both physical and figurative—that may interfere with an organization's operations and objectives" (Kenton 2019).

Key takeaways from these definitions include:

- ERM is applied in a strategy setting.
- It is applied across the enterprise or organization.

- It is part of the organization's decision-making process.
- It must add value in helping the library manage risk more effectively and efficiently.

Other key concepts of ERM include risk appetite, risk altitude, and risk owner.

What Is Risk Appetite?

Risk appetite is defined as that level of risk an organization is willing to accept in order to achieve its objectives. Risk appetite should be set at the board level.

What Is Risk Altitude?

The concept of risk altitude recognizes that not all risks are created equal. Not all risks should be handled at one level within the library. For example, operational risk is best managed at the operations level, while strategic risks are best managed at the board level. The key takeaway here is that for risk management to be effective and efficient, risks need to be assigned to the administrative level in the library that is best equipped for their identification, evaluation, and implementation. Risks are not isolated concepts, but rather have interactions and connections across the library.

What Is a Risk Owner?

The term risk owner can have several definitions. In one definition, the risk owner is the person in an organization who is ultimately accountable for making sure that risk is managed appropriately. This is usually a person at the senior management level who coordinates efforts to lessen and manage the risks with the various individuals who are directly responsible for the day-to-day management of each identifiable risk. In another definition, all of these individuals are risk owners, since they "own" that part of the risk whose management they are responsible for. They typically will be the individual responsible for the "doing." Because risk owners are the "doers," their insight and perspective is very important in providing valuable information, such as risk identification and evaluation or feedback on implementation and operational activities.

ERM IMPLEMENTATION STRATEGIES

One of the most challenging tasks in any organization, including a library, is how to implement an ERM framework. Instead of creating a separate ERM framework, with a separate reporting structure and committees, consider how to weave ERM into your library's existing decision-making and management structures.

1. ERM is best applied in a strategy setting.

Let's recall our key takeaways from the ERM definitions. ERM is best applied in strategic planning, or a "strategy setting." A board of trustees will usually undergo a strategy-setting exercise every three to five years. Typically, strategy planning involves "big picture" discussions.

When was the last time your board undertook a strategy-setting exercise? When was the last time your board assessed its current strategy? If you are at the stage where the board is considering a strategy-planning agenda item, this is an opportunity to introduce ERM concepts as part of that agenda item.

In preparation for this board activity, consider ensuring that there is adequate discussion around the strengths and weaknesses of a proposed risk management strategy. Ensure that possible barriers or challenges to successfully implementing that strategy are identified and that possible plans are discussed to overcome those barriers or challenges. Plans may include identifying additional resources that could be made available or acquired.

2. ERM needs to be applied across an enterprise.

Recall our second takeaway from the ERM definitions—that ERM needs to be applied across the enterprise or library.

Once the board has completed its strategic planning, which hopefully includes plans or resources that could be implemented to overcome identified barriers or challenges, how are these strategic goals communicated to both managers and front-line employees of the library?

Are the strategic goals and plans clearly understood by all?

Are sufficient resources and support provided to ensure success?

Is it clearly understood what "success" looks like?

In implementing the board's strategic goals, do managers and supervisors identify risks associated with that implementation? Do they identify roadblocks or challenges to ensure successful completion? Do they identify plans to manage the risks?

Does decision-making align with the strategic plan?

And most importantly, how are risk identification and feedback communicated?

3. ERM is part of the decision-making process.

In order for the library to provide "assurance that it can meet its objectives," ERM needs to be part of the decision-making process. ERM is at its core, a management process.

Consider who the decision-makers in your organization are. Consider who has authority and who has responsibility. How are projects and initiatives managed? How are the library's facilities managed? Risk owners, a concept introduced above, are typically those individuals who are best placed to identify risks, evaluate them, and provide feedback on whether the risk treatment strategies are effective.

4. ERM adds value.

It is not enough simply that risks are identified. More importantly, it is what is done with that information that adds value and provides assurance that the library can meet its objectives. There need to be functional and healthy feedback loops.

How do front-line staff communicate risk identification and evaluation to their managers? And in turn, how do managers communicate important risk information to senior administrators, and then how is important risk information communicated to the board level? If feedback loops are broken, dysfunctional, or ineffective, then decision-makers, risk owners, and board members will not have the accurate risk information they need in order to make informed decisions.

WHAT ABOUT THAT RISK COMMITTEE?

Your library may already be part of an ERM framework, or may already have a Risk Committee, or may be thinking of establishing a risk committee. Typically, a risk committee is formed so that risks can be identified and evaluated. The formation of a risk committee is one of the most obvious ways to demonstrate that an ERM framework is being followed. As we discussed above, ERM is really a management/decision-making framework. Management frameworks already exist within the library. It really doesn't make much sense to add an existing structure to something that exists. Should you decide to proceed with a risk committee, here are some considerations:

Committee membership: Consider who should be a member of the committee. Good management means ensuring that the "right people are at the table." Consider committee appointments for a certain defined length of time.

Committee size: The larger the size of the committee, the more unwieldly and cumbersome it is. Quality is better than quantity.

Scope: Ensure that your risk committee has a defined scope. This assists in guarding against mission creep. Scope can also include how long a committee needs to be in existence.

Frequency of meeting: Setting in advance the frequency of meeting will depend on the committee's scope.

Deliverables: The committee's scope should include clearly defined deliverables. An example of a deliverable would be to complete a report of all actions and decisions taken by the committee, and submit it to the board.

Value: The value that a risk committee should bring to the library, or any organization, will depend on its clearly defined scope and its deliverables. There should always be an ongoing self-assessment by committee members on whether the existence of the committee is adding value to the library. In an ERM context, value could be defined as: "Does this committee assist decision-makers in making more informed decisions? Does it assist in the overall management of the Library?"

But before creating a risk committee, consider your current management framework and using existing management frameworks to embed ERM practices, rather than creating duplicative structures.

ERM AND LIBRARIES—AN EXAMPLE

The Rainbow Library is our hypothetical library example. This is a highly simplified example of ERM in action. In this example, the Rainbow Library does not have a risk committee, but instead has opted to integrate ERM principles into its overall management structure. (Management frameworks typically include three actions or stages: assess, plan, and implement.)

Rainbow Library's strategic planning process involves a number of different steps where the library director, and her management team, requested feedback from staff and key stakeholders. This feedback had been provided to the board to finalize and adopt the library's strategic plan. In its recent strategic planning session, the board adopted the following strategic goals:

1. Partner to promote and enhance learning
2. Improve access to materials and services
3. Expand community connections

Since ERM is embedded in the overall management of the Rainbow Library, the board was comfortable in identifying strategic risks as part of its strategic planning process. During this planning session, the board engaged in some frank and open discussions about possible challenges and roadblocks. These challenges and roadblocks included the following: in order to "promote and enhance learning," more funding was needed to update and expand the square footage of learning spaces in the library building. In addition, concerns were expressed about the current IT infrastructure's capacity to support "improved access to materials and services." For "expanding community connections," the board reviewed its fundraising targets, and reviewed last year's report on library events and outreach programs. This report highlighted that Rainbow Library was currently at capacity, and its facilities were old and outdated.

The board identified the following strategic risk: a failure to meet funding/capital targets to fund facility and technology upgrades. In order to manage this risk, the board discussed its funding strategies and targets. After discussion, the board was reasonably satisfied that it would meet its capital needs through meeting its funding targets from private, foundation, and corporate sources.

After the board meeting, the director of Rainbow Library called a meeting of her management team to discuss the strategic goals that the board finalized, including information provided to the board about the facilities, the IT infrastructure, and additional fundraising.

Facilities: The facilities manager again repeated that the current facilities were in much need of upgrading. He expressed concerns about the board's strategic goals and asked the director about the funding for much-needed upgrades. Because the board had embedded ERM into its strategic planning, the director was able to share with the facilities manager how much funding there would be for the needed upgrades. Because the Rainbow Library has a functional management framework that actively encourages (and empowers) feedback, the director asks the facilities manager to provide an update of his assessment of the scope and potential cost of the upgrades. She in turn can take that information back to the board, as well as to the director of donor relations.

Technology: The IT manager discussed her concerns. Again, because Rainbow's board had identified the risks associated with its strategic plans, the operational leaders (facilities and IT) were able to connect with the director of donor relations and share with her their funding needs.

The director of donor relations does have some concerns about the board's strategic plans. She connects with the facilities and IT managers to determine their funding needs to coordinate her gift-giving strategy. Table 1.1 delineates goals of ERM along with challenges and risks that may be encountered in meeting those goals, strategies, and actions to overcome challenges and risks identified and describes the person responsible for identifying the resources necessary to attain the goals enumerated.

TABLE 1.1

Risk Matrix

Strategic Goal	Challenges/Risks	Strategies/Actions	Risk Owners
Partner to promote and enhance learning	Aging facility. Lack of space or usable square footage	Facility report prepared. Identifies facility upgrades and enhancements and provides estimated budget.	Library director Facility manager Budget and Finance Board
Improve access to materials and services	Current IT infrastructure capacity inadequate to support improved access	Connect with IT manager to determine resources needed to upgrade IT infrastructure.	Library director IT Budget and Finance Board
Expand community connections	Failure to meet funding/capital targets to fund facility and technology upgrades	Library to implement capital campaign, and target marketing around fundraising for strategic goals.	Library director Donor Relations Budget and Finance Board

Good management frameworks, with functional teams and feedback mechanisms, are hard work. They do not come easily. The Rainbow Library example assumes that teams and feedback mechanisms are functional.

2
Risk Identification

Risk identification is a search for the potential sources of losses or opportunities. Insurable risks are those risks for which insurance can be purchased in order to finance the potential risk of loss. This chapter contains several categories and areas to consider for insurable hazards and risks of loss. It also includes a brief explanation of the circumstances or events that are likely to cause loss. We briefly discuss risks as opportunities, non-insurable risks, and the concept of risk altitudes.

The library should develop a systematic approach to risk identification that might include any or all of the following tools:

- a facility inspection by the library's staff
- the insurance company's inspection reports
- a review of the library's past losses
- a risk analysis questionnaire
- an operations flow chart
- analysis of financial statements
- a review of contracts and leases the library has signed

- a review of local and state statutes that impose duties on the library relative to the general public, such as state statutes related to workers' compensation insurance, or local statutes related to the library's obligation to provide free and clear access to its premises and services
- a review of new programming, and other new initiatives

The more of these tools the library utilizes, the more thorough the identification of potential risks of loss will be. Using all the tools available will allow the library to develop the most complete risk identification. It is important to note that this step can be ongoing and continuous. The library may use one or more of the tools to get started and add to the risk identification process over time. It is also important to keep in mind that this process should be utilized any time new operations are undertaken that might entail new risks, such as the introduction of new programs that increase the participation of the general public on the library's premises, or renovations to existing library facilities or the addition of new facilities.

MAJOR AREAS OF RISK OF LOSS

The library must identify risks from

- physical damage to, or loss of, library property, including buildings, library books and other materials, equipment, and vehicles;
- liability losses arising from claims or lawsuits alleging negligence in the operation of the library;
- losses resulting from injury to library staff;
- financial losses arising from unlawful acts; and
- loss of reputation.

PROPERTY

In most instances, virtually all property owned by, leased to, or in the care, custody, or control of the library can be damaged, destroyed, or lost in the course of library operations due to any number of causes. The sections and subsections that follow will cover the major items of property the library owns, uses, controls, or has responsibility for, and whose loss or damage could result in financial loss, or a disruption of the library's operations.

In the risk identification process, the library will list all property for which it is responsible in each category. When identifying the types of property that are potentially subject to loss, it is common to separate the property into two categories: real property and personal property. (The issues of appraisal and valuation of tangible property are discussed in chapter 3.)

REAL PROPERTY

- Buildings: This category comprises all buildings owned or leased by the library, including buildings under construction, office facilities, book storage facilities, and garages. It also includes permanently affixed machinery, such as equipment used to maintain or service the building, including boilers and HVAC systems. Fire extinguishing equipment; appliances used for refrigeration, ventilation, cooking, and dishwashing; and certain outdoor fixtures, such as a flagpole, book returns, and a sign attached to the library building, also fall into this category. When categorizing leased property, the library must first determine whether the lease requires the library or the owner to be responsible for damage or destruction of the property.
- Real property includes landscaping, but not the land itself.

PERSONAL PROPERTY

Personal property is generally considered all property that is movable and not permanently affixed to the buildings and the land. In the library, it includes such items as the following:

- books and other collection materials, including periodicals, manuscripts, films, prints, audio and video tapes, sound recordings, maps, digital facsimiles, drawings, artwork, and all other materials intended for the use of library patrons
- furniture and fixtures, including desks, chairs, lamps and other lighting, filing cabinets, bookstacks, shelving, public-access computers, microform readers and printers, listening stations, and photocopiers
- machinery and equipment other than that permanently affixed to a building or used to maintain or service the building (This category may embrace a wide variety of property, including office machines, copier machines, microform readers and printers, scanners, digital cameras, projection machines, and other equipment.)
- electronic data-processing (EDP) equipment, including computer hardware and software

- electronic data, including library records, indexes, and possibly the online catalog maintained on digital/electronic storage media
- fine art, paintings, antiques, rare books, manuscripts, collections of letters and other personal papers, and other rare, unique, or irreplaceable items
- valuable papers and records, including records that have a value in excess of the actual tangible value of the cost of paper plus the cost of transcribing (These may include library catalogs [if the catalog is not electronic] and other library records, such as financial and accounting records.)
- consumable supplies and materials, such as office stationery, envelopes, library supplies, and janitorial supplies
- accounts receivable
- promotional displays, informational signs, and exhibits
- cash and negotiable instruments
- motor vehicles and bookmobiles
- the property of others, including property belonging to the library's employees and books on loan (This category may encompass a large variety of property, such as office machines, photocopiers, scanners, and other equipment that has been loaned or leased by the library rather than being owned outright by it. The responsibility of the library for these items should be clearly stated in the loan or lease agreement or contract related to the equipment.)

PROPERTY PERILS

Property can be lost, damaged, or destroyed by virtually any cause. However, many causes of loss occur in the ordinary course of business and are not risks with which risk management is generally concerned. Risk management generally focuses on types of losses that can be prevented or minimized and those that can be financed, either by the library itself or by a third party (either a contracting party or a commercial insurer). From a risk management perspective, the following is a list of common perils to which the library's property may be subject:

- fire and lightning
- riot, explosion, vehicle damage, smoke, hail, aircraft damage, and windstorm (including hurricanes and tornadoes)
- vandalism and malicious mischief
- sprinkler leakage

- water damage from defective plumbing, heating, or air-conditioning systems
- collapse of buildings or structures
- glass breakage
- burglary, theft, robbery
- boiler and machinery
- property in transit
- earthquake
- flood, backed-up sewers, surface waters
- terrorism

OTHER PROPERTY RISKS

Improvements and Betterments

This pertains to improvements made in a leased building, such as permanent fixtures, new plumbing facilities, and the like, which have been made by the library as the tenant under a current lease. In every case, the library should review the lease to determine whether the landlord has an obligation to replace the improvements and betterments in the event of loss or damage. If the landlord does not have this legal obligation, the library has two risks of loss:

- the cost of replacing the improvements if they are damaged or destroyed in order to continue to use the building
- the unamortized portion of the improvements and betterments or their use value for the unexpired terms of the lease, should the landlord cancel the lease as a result of the loss or damage

Business Interruption

Business interruptions include lost revenue and continuing expenses that will be incurred by the library in the event of a loss that causes the library to interrupt its operations or to discontinue some or all its services.

Extra Expenses

Extra expenses are funds in excess of normal operating costs that become necessary to continue operations if the library's facilities are damaged or destroyed. An indirect loss can result from serious damage to library property in the form of extra or additional expense if the library desires to continue its services at temporary locations. The library should determine in advance whether it will need an extra fund to continue operating at temporary locations in the event of a catastrophe. If so, the library should determine the amount of extra or unusual expenses that might be necessary to continue operation, and for what period of time.

LIABILITY

In addition to loss involving library-owned property, the library may suffer financial loss related to injuries to people or damage to non-owned or leased property that occurs as a result of the library's operations and for which the library is responsible, either due to the negligence of library employees or agents in conducting library business or due to the statutory or regulatory imposition of responsibility. Some of the most common sources of liability risks are listed below.

Premises

Premises includes the building, grounds, and leased property. The liability of the library may result from negligent maintenance of the premises that results in an injury to a third party. For example, poorly lit steps, water on the floor, cracks on sidewalks, dimly lit parking facilities, incomplete snow removal, and tripping hazards may lead to liability as all of these could result in an injury to a third party.

Operations or Activities

Operations or activities includes the actions of board members, officers, employees, agents, and volunteers. Many libraries have moved beyond reading and lending books as their only activities. Cafés, exercise and dance classes, arts and crafts programs, stage and musical performances, and even after-school care are all part of the offerings at many libraries. While these activities can enhance the value of the library experience, they also create additional exposures. Coffee served in the café may burn someone, negligent dance instruction can lead to an injured participant, and negligent supervision in arts and crafts programs can lead to injury.

Contracts or Leases

Contracts or leases are arrangements in which the library has agreed to indemnify or hold harmless the other party for liability for injuries arising out of the contract. (In the case of new construction, the library may be the beneficiary of such a clause wherein the contractor agrees to hold harmless the library. Chapter 7 discusses this concept in greater detail.)

Autos, Trucks, Mobile Equipment, and Bookmobiles

Autos, trucks, mobile equipment, and bookmobiles includes vehicles owned, leased, or hired by the library, as well as vehicles owned by others that are being driven on library business.

INTENTIONAL TORTS

Torts are civil wrongs. In the course of library business, any number of intentional torts may subject the library to liability. The library should consider in its risk identification process the risk of loss due to libel, slander, invasion of privacy (including while using electronic equipment and computers), assault, battery, false arrest, or trespass. There are some steps you can take to protect your library. For example, including statements on public computers with directions on how to maintain privacy and rules for use may provide tort protection. Training security officers in proper conduct will assist in tort protection against assault and battery.

DIRECTORS' OR TRUSTEES' AND OFFICERS' LIABILITY

Directors, trustees, and officers are also subject to liability risk. In the case of a nonprofit corporation or a public (governmental or quasi-governmental) body, a similar action might be brought by a member or by a citizen whom the corporation or public body is organized to serve. For example, budget constraints might lead to a reduction in communities served by bookmobiles, leading a community to file an action against the library's board.

EMPLOYMENT PRACTICES LIABILITY

Library boards may have to face suits by employees who claim there has been a violation of their civil rights in hiring, promotion, or in a wrongful discharge based on race, gender, sexual orientation, religion, national origin, or other characteristics.

FIDUCIARY LIABILITY

Fiduciary liability is the risk of the library to responsibly and ethically handle funds entrusted to it.

EMPLOYEE BENEFITS LIABILITY

Employee benefits liability arises from the administration of a benefit policy for an entity's employees. An example of this type of liability would be neglecting to properly inform an employee of—or failing to register an employee for—benefits, causing the employee to suffer financial loss in the future.

CYBER LIABILITY

Cyber liability is a relatively new exposure that arises from the risks of conducting operations over the internet or networks or from using electronic storage technology. Various insurance policies are available for cyber liability. Some policies also include coverage for privacy compliance penalties. An example of this would be if the library's databases are breached and patrons' or employees' personal protected information is stolen.

LIABILITY RISKS

Bodily Injury (BI)

This category of risk includes sickness, disease, death, or mental injury allegedly suffered by library patrons or members of the general public as a result of negligence by library staff or any other person for whom the library is responsible.

Property Damage (PD)

These risks relate to physical injury to, or destruction of, tangible property, including loss of use thereof, incurred as a result of a claim of negligence in library operations.

Personal Injury (PI)

These risks involve libel, slander, defamation, or violation of privacy rights; false arrest, detention or imprisonment, or malicious prosecution; discrimination; or deprivation, violation, or infringement of rights.

OTHER RISKS

Injury to Employees

The risks to be considered here are injuries suffered by employees in the course of their employment. Exposure includes medical expenses, salary continuance, permanent or temporary disability, loss of limb(s), rehabilitation, and death.

Employee Dishonesty Risks

These risks relate to dishonest, fraudulent, or criminal acts committed by library employees that may result in financial loss to the library. Examples include the unlawful electronic transfer of library funds and theft from the library's petty cash fund. These risks are not limited to the library's treasurer or controller or even those in a supervisory capacity. The risk involves loss of property as well as money, and even those not directly responsible for library funds may discover ways to defraud the library.

Special Events

Special events can be sources of significant risks and include the following risks:

- sale and consumption of alcohol
- inadequate public health controls when serving food to guests
- size of crowds
- poor signage (exits, etc.)
- slippery surfaces
- weather conditions (heat, cold, rain, wind)
- location not designated for such an event
- event-related controversies
- lack of adequate parking lot lighting and security
- lack of an evacuation plan
- slow emergency response

Risk as Opportunity

Insurable risks are those risks that cause an adverse impact should they occur. However, in our definition of enterprise risk management earlier, risks do not always have an adverse impact. Risks may be an uncertain opportunity which, if it occurs, may have a positive impact on the entity. For example, the library wishes to grow its patron bequest program. The uncertainty is that the program may or may not be successful. Risk or opportunity identification is an important exercise for the library to undertake. Risk identification of insurable risk assists with determining the size and design of an insurance program for the library. However, it is important for discussions around risk identification to also focus on other types of risks.

NON-INSURABLE RISKS

Risks that are non-insurable may still need to be identified and managed in order to prevent these risks from having an adverse impact to the library's mission and operations. Examples of such non-insurable risks include reputational risks; aging and deteriorating infrastructure; the deterioration of library collections based on age, and wear and tear; and compliance or regulatory risks.

3
Risk Quantification and Evaluation

In matters of risk management and insurance, knowledge is a source of added security. It is the key element in the risk management and insurance program for any library. Chapter 1 outlined the steps in the risk management process. This chapter further explores the second step, risk quantification and evaluation.

Risk quantification involves assessing, both objectively and subjectively, the potential impact of risks. If a library is to make well-informed decisions, it is critical not only to identify property and operations that present risks of loss, but also to evaluate the risks and magnitude of all the library's assets, including physical property and financial assets. Ultimately, decisions regarding risk financing, including insurance, will depend on the accurate valuation of assets, especially library collections. Not only must the library determine the value of its collections, it also must identify which portions of a collection need to be restored most quickly following an interruption in service. For example, in an academic library, it may be most critical to ensure that the reserve collection, which contains required reading for students, is first back in service. In a public library, it may be more important to ensure that the children's collection is first to resume service following an interruption.

The responsibility of attaching value to the library's specific collections rests predominantly with the library staff. This can be challenging. The next section provides a broad overview of how to establish accurate values for the library's property, both real and personal. The section also includes a methodology for valuing library collections, likely the highest valued property.

PROPERTY

If the library has not determined how much it will cost to replace damaged or destroyed property, it is without a complete measure of its property exposures. (The types of property, real and personal, were defined in chapter 2.) First and foremost, it is important to note that the purchase price of the library's physical assets has very little to do with the assessment of their value to the library in the event of a loss. Likewise, any recording of assets that lists them by original cost minus depreciation will not give an accurate picture of the value of that property in the event of loss or damage.

Instead, risk management and insurance rely on two other concepts to determine value. The first is actual cash value (ACV), which is defined as the replacement cost at the time of loss less depreciation. This concept also takes inflation into consideration. ACV does not necessarily result in lower values, as many believe. ACV values may actually increase if the rate of inflation exceeds the rate of depreciation. However, the impact of depreciation, which accounts for wear and tear and economic obsolescence, often results in a substantial loss of asset value. The deduction for depreciation will obligate the library to make up the difference to restore the property to its original condition, which is why most property should be valued on a replacement-cost basis.

Replacement cost is simply the cost of replacing all library-owned and leased property new at current prices. These replacement costs, replacement times, and repair times are calculated on a non-expedited basis in the regular course of business, including time to order, receive, and process replacement books. This method of quantifying all property identified in the first step of the risk management process will give the library the most accurate picture of the potential for loss.

REAL PROPERTY VALUATION

Buildings

Replacement cost, as applied to buildings, denotes the cost of replacing a complete structure and permanently affixed machinery, including equipment used to maintain or service the building. It includes the entire building: superstructure; foundations; finish work (case and cabinet work, ceiling, wall, and floor coverings, painting); elevators; heating, ventilation, and air condition-ing (HVAC) equipment; lighting, wiring, and electrical service equipment; fire protection devices (automatic sprinklers, valves, pumps); plumbing fixtures and piping; and other building service and utility equipment, such as fire-ex-tinguishing equipment, appliances used for refrigeration, ventilation, cook-ing, and certain outdoor fixtures (a flagpole or a sign attached to a building, for instance). Also included are other permanent items, such as landscaping, pavement, fencing, underground piping and wiring, and retaining walls.

All labor costs are estimated at prevailing union rates. Additionally, the replacement cost for buildings includes costs for general or unusual condi-tions, such as special load-bearing requirements for bookstacks, architect's and engineer's fees, permits, and other direct and indirect costs necessary for reproducing the building.

Buildings on the National Register of Historic Places, or that have value beyond their ordinary replacement cost, will require specialized knowledge regarding what can or must be done in the event of damage. This will require input beyond the library staff, including architects and engineers who special-ize in restoring these structures.

Real property values assigned to library buildings also should recognize the quality of finishes, partitions, and plumbing.

Real property values should exclude excavation or other site work and be based on the total floor area of all floors, measured from outside wall to out-side wall (also referred to as the gross floor area). This measurement should be taken for all floors, including basements, finished attics, penthouses, and those mezzanines, galleries, and platforms where the individual floor area is 10 percent or more of the footprint of the building.

Structures that are not buildings, such as water towers, should be included as real property. The values for any new buildings and additions under con-struction also should be included.

When estimating a building's value, the library should consult a construc-tion cost guide, a useful reference in determining the value per-square-foot for the building structure. Many insurance companies have guides that can be useful in establishing values for library buildings. These guides help the library determine value that reflects the building's construction, uniqueness of design, and geographic area, and that takes into consideration the end-use of the building and associated costs, such as construction needed to increase the floor-load capacity. Square footage and special construction, such as addi-tional load bearing for bookstacks, should be documented and updated from the construction cost guides at least every five years.

The Library and Book Trade Almanac (formerly The Bowker Annual) pro-vides many different reports. Among them is a table of "New Public Library Buildings," listed by state and by community within each state. This table can be a useful reference to help the library estimate average construction costs for library buildings within the geographical area. Note that construction costs can vary greatly depending on the location and the type of library. For example, in 2019 a new library in Alabama cost $212 per square foot, while a new library in California cost $692 per square foot. A new library in Arlington, Texas, cost $234 per square foot, while a new library in Austin, Texas, cost $471 per square foot. Similar information is available for academic library buildings.

Appraisals

One of the best ways to obtain accurate property and replacement values is to have an appraisal firm conduct an on-site field appraisal. Using blueprints or actual field measurements, the appraiser will determine the quantities and sizes of the building's components and materials. When blueprints are not available and components are situated too high to be measured, appraisers will estimate sizes by comparing them to known component sizes (bricks, masonry units, wood or steel members, ladder rungs, and so on). These techniques have produced reliable, accurate estimates.

The appraiser then discerns the replacement value of buildings and other structures by applying unit costs of the individual construction materials in place to the quantities established by the field measurements and blueprints. Costs are adjusted by region to account for local labor and material cost variances. Appraisers do not factor in costs to conform to building codes, ordinances, or other legal restrictions; the cost of demolition in connection with reconstruction; or the removal of destroyed property.

See appendix A, "Risk Management and Insurance Resources," for more information.

Improvements and Betterments in Leased Buildings

The valuation should be determined in the same manner as for buildings. If the landlord has the obligation of replacement, but also has the option of lease cancellation in the event of a loss, the measure of risk for the library usually will be the unamortized leasehold value; that is, that proportion of the original cost to the library for the improvements as represented by the unexpired portion of the lease.

PERSONAL PROPERTY VALUATION

The owned contents of the library building (personal property) can generally be divided into four categories for valuation:

- furniture, including bookstacks and specialized storage, such as flat files for poster and map storage
- business operations information
- electronic data processing equipment (EDP)
- physical collections

Physical collections (which include books, maps, audio-visual materials, journals, manuscripts, and rare materials), because they tend to include both older and new materials, often are the most difficult to value. Within collections, the distinction between general circulating collections and special or rare materials also should be noted for valuation purposes.

The library staff is often better prepared than a general appraiser to take responsibility for placing a value on library collections. In the case of vehicles, furniture, exhibits, consumables, office equipment, copiers, readers, printers, and computers, the replacement value can be determined through an inventory. Replacement costs for personal property include the cost of replacing all the facility's contents with the same or similar new items, as well as fees for shipping and installation, equipment and materials, testing and commissioning, and warranty and service. The replacement time includes engineering and design, date of order to date of shipment, normal transportation time, installation time, and testing and commissioning periods, all to be calculated at the time of loss. A good inventory control practice is essential for verifying materials destroyed in a loss. It is vital to update the inventory as equipment is replaced or upgraded in order to provide accurate records for valuation.

As with books, computers and most software are considered standard library contents. Examples include publicly accessible computers, software, computer files, printers, 3D printers, and online catalogs. An up-to-date inventory of computer hardware and software also is important to an effective valuation because libraries now depend on computers to access titles in electronic formats.

All equipment lease agreements, such as those for copiers or computers, should clearly state the responsible party in the event of loss. If the library is the responsible party, it must update the valuation of leased equipment. On-loan materials also fall under this category, and interlibrary loan material agreements should clearly state the responsible party in the event of loss. If the library is responsible for loaned materials, these items should be included in its inventory and valuation. (If the patron is responsible for any loss or damage, libraries should make that clear at the time of the borrowing.)

A detailed inventory that includes valuations for all property is essential both for arriving at an accurate risk assessment and for establishing or proving a loss. The more detailed the description of each item, the easier it is to establish its value at the time of loss. However, it is not necessary to list minor items. Instead, these usually can be grouped together when the total amount is not large.

Suggested methods of establishing the base value are as follows:

- If the original cost and year of purchase are available, values can be trended from cost tables to current prices, providing the original purchase information is not older than the maximum useful life of the trends. In the case of a relatively new library, original purchase records may be readily available. Again, many insurance companies can provide cost trend tables.
- The librarian or an assistant can make an inventory and price each item or each group of items from current catalogs. Installation costs for communications equipment that is not a part of the building value and for EDP equipment should be included.

Values for buildings and contents alike should be brought up to date annually using the latest cost indices. For updating replacement cost values, the library may refer to insurance carriers or to Marshall and Swift (see appendix A).

Appraisals

An appraiser hired to do a real property valuation also can be retained to inspect and individually list contents of furniture and business operations information. Typically, appraisers list enough information about the equipment so its replacement cost may be properly researched upon return to their office. Relatively low-value, high-quantity items, such as furniture, fixtures, small machinery and equipment, and personal computers, are grouped and totaled. In the office, equipment replacement prices are researched and totaled. To the new price of the equipment, a value is added to cover freight, taxes, foundation, and installation. Also included, if necessary, is value to cover unusual conditions that would be encountered in association with acquiring and installing equipment, such as obtaining licenses, certification, and so on. These are also included to develop the full replacement value.

Appraisals conducted for general insurance purposes, including buildings and contents, typically will value items such as fine art, rare books, historical artifacts, archival documents, paintings, and sculptures at their decorative, functional value purpose only—not at replacement cost. A specialized appraisal is needed to determine the replacement costs for these library properties. For more information about specialized appraisal services, see appendix A.

BOOKS AND LIBRARY MATERIALS

For general library collections and rare materials, usually the administrator can best assess replacement value using standard library tools that are unfamiliar to insurance appraisers. General collections can be valued by setting an average value within a subject area. For special or rare collections, individual pieces above a certain amount should be scheduled with values set by title or by piece or collection.

General Collections: Books and Periodicals

The majority of libraries today use some sort of online catalog for documenting collections and providing circulation services and access for the public. In most cases, these online systems can provide a wealth of information about the collection, which can be used by librarians for valuation. Because material value varies greatly by subject and because replacement value is far different from purchase price after a certain age, even circulating collections can be undervalued. Most libraries keep statistics on the total number of pieces in a collection for annual reports and other statistical reporting. However, more granularity is necessary to assure accurate valuation if the collections cover more than one subject area or if the collection spans a long period of copyright dates. For additional resources, please see the Library of Congress website's section on emergency management at www.loc.gov/preservation/emergprep.

Book dealers and library book jobbers can provide a wealth of information about the current price of materials by subject. This information, coupled with reports acquired through the online catalog, can provide a useful and highly accurate valuation. Because most losses are partial, the grouping of collections by location, in addition to subject, is important to consider in the valuation. In the case of a partial loss to the most expensive portion of the collection, the importance of accurate valuation by location and subject is obvious.

Determining the most likely fire scenario will help a library determine the best method for grouping materials. For example, separating the collection by building wing is recommended in cases where the library is one multistory building yet houses two separate heating and cooling units. This separation is suggested because the most likely fire scenario would result in partial loss on multiple floors in only one wing, rather than in both wings of the building.

Determining the value of library collections is a formidable task. Many municipalities have large library buildings with extensive general collections, while others also maintain additional collections in neighborhood libraries and bookmobiles. The total number of items involved is so great that individual pricing is not practical. The solution is to develop an average value for each category within each location. Generally, the better categorized the collection, the more accurate the values.

Here are some tips to help the library reach an accurate determination of collection values:

- Divide monograph titles from serial titles to estimate values
  by titles. Using the online catalog, determine the number of

monograph titles per call number division and then do the same
for serial titles.

- Compile a physical volume count for serials in addition to the title
count. Taking an average number of physical volumes per title
and by subject is a good method for determining a per-volume
replacement value for serial titles.
- Sort the collection by format and location using the online
catalog. This allows the library to determine the values for such
formats as audiotapes and DVDs separately from book formats.
- Include the cost of processing in the replacement cost estimate.
The cost of ordering, processing, and shelving a library volume
varies widely across the country because of different salary scales
for staff.

Most libraries have a fairly accurate count of the number of volumes in their
collection, but the number of volumes broken down into format (periodical,
monograph, or nonprint) within each subject is sometimes unknown. Online
catalogs of library holdings often provide the number of held titles, but they
generally do not give a volume count. If a collection has bar codes used for dis-
charging and charging materials to patrons, then a more accurate number of
physical volumes can be determined. In the past, volume and title counts were
difficult to determine. Today's library management systems allow this task to
be accomplished more efficiently.

The breakdown of volumes by subject is important to determine the value
of a general collection. Many book jobbers can provide average cost by subject
and, in some cases, such values are provided free on websites. The Library and
Book Trade Almanac (formerly The Bowker Annual) published by Information Today publishes prices of U.S. and foreign-published materials by subject area, as well as serials, e-books, and other media. ALCTS, which is now
part of Core, publishes an annual price list of U.S. and foreign publications
for the past and current price indexes. (See www.ala.org/alcts/resources/
collect/serials/spi; check for new website name after 2021.) GOBI Library
Solutions provides "New Title Reports—Publishers Profiles in the U.S." (See
www.gobi3.com/StaticContent/GOBIContent/YBP/Private/Help/Pages/
newtitlereport_us.html.)

Once a complete valuation has been made for a collection, new volumes
can be added each year. However, the library should periodically revalue the
collection to estimate accurately the replacement costs of materials using current pricing. It is suggested that a valuation be completed every five years. In
addition, the library should conduct an annual review to determine the total
number of items in each category of books and library materials, and to apply
appropriate average prices to each. Normally, this entails an adjustment of the
previous year's inventory by additions and deletions.

The following are the values of various contents found in different libraries. These are not absolute amounts, but they give the library an indication of the figures with which it will be working in the valuation.

Periodicals

Below are some 2019 values for periodical subscriptions according to the Library and Book Trade Almanac. Note the large differences in prices by subject:

- average periodical price, agriculture: $1,080.51
- general interest periodicals: $134.98
- history: $353.43
- health sciences: $1,907.29
- physical education and recreation: $176.45

Books

Hardcover book values for 2018 are nearly as varied:

- average hardcover book price: $94.45
- arts: $74.87
- technology: $200.03
- foreign language study: $117.66
- young adult: $35.65
- fiction: $29.45
- sports, recreation: $53.02
- travel: $40.90
- other formats:
  - e-books: $114.61
  - audiobooks vary: crafts $51.31; foreign language $210.10

Note that all sources give average prices for various categories of materials. When using these figures as a basis for valuation, the library should keep these points in mind:

- The list prices of newly published materials are average retail prices. Adjustments must be made for a variety of factors, including geographic price variations, shipping and handling charges, and any discounts available to the library.
- The library's costs of processing and reshelving are not included in these prices.
- The Library and Book Trade Almanac is only one guide that may be useful. Librarians in special libraries, such as law, medicine, and

engineering, may get assistance directly from publishers in those fields.

- Over a period of several years, librarians who wish to analyze their own purchases may be able to rely on their own average costs or make adjustments to the costs in the *Library and Book Trade Almanac* or other reference sources based on their purchases.
- Average discounts being realized by the library in its purchases should be included in the calculation.
- The library should reduce the collection's total value by an amount representing the estimated value of books and library materials out on loan.

Many library book companies now maintain websites with useful breakdowns of cost by subject. Often, these breakdowns are much more detailed than what was once available in the Library and Book Trade Almanac. One such example is GOBI Library Solutions (see https://gobi.ebsco.com/about). The Library of Congress provides freely accessible information that lists valuations by call number area. (See their website www.loc.gov/preservation/emergprep/.) Pairing this with the number of volumes in each call number category using a report or search function in the online catalog can provide a very detailed valuation. However, as noted above, before the library begins a valuation by subject, it should first divide the collection by location.

A software package to calculate the accumulated numbers of volumes and the per-unit value can provide a much more accurate replacement value. While this method works well for monograph titles, serials require a slightly different method. For monograph titles, multivolume sets are assumed to be figured into the cost breakdown by call number. For serial collections, the acquisitions module of the online catalog often can be used to determine the current subscription price as well as the number of titles and the volume count. These three reports can provide a reasonable average price for serials within classification breakdowns like the method given for monograph titles. Again, dividing the values by location is useful in the event of a partial loss.

Government Documents

International, state, and local government documents may come to the library through various channels that include for free and for-fee services such as exchange or deposit programs, subscriptions, or mailing lists maintained by the agency, or through commercial vendors.

U.S. Federal Government documents may come free of charge to the library through a library's official designation as a member of the Federal Depository Library Program (FDLP). As members of the FDLP, libraries are asked to insure their FDLP collections against loss using the same risk assessment and insurance policy used for their general collections. The U.S. Government Publishing Office (GPO) is not in a position to provide guidance regarding the appropriate formula for establishing the level of coverage for the documents it publishes. Many depository libraries base their insurance estimates on the cost of replacing a similar number of volumes from their commercially acquired collections. In this case, a blanket policy may therefore be sufficient. Depository libraries should be aware that it is important to understand the language found in their insurance policy to ensure that their government documents collection is properly insured. The U.S. government retains ownership of all FDLP members' depository collections. Therefore, the language used to describe the coverage for FDLP members' collections should refer to collections "shelved" or "housed" within the library rather than collections owned by the library. If the language in the policy describes coverage based on collection ownership, the FDLP collection may unfortunately be excluded from the library's policy.

The GPO now provides a new tool for FDLP libraries, FDLP eXchange, to use when they want to replace a portion of their collection lost through a disaster by requesting replacement volumes or sharing their collection "needs." The FDLP eXchange is accessible from www.fdlp.gov/fdlp-exchange.

Maps, posters, and photographs may also be part of the general collection. The library should include their location and replacement value in the totals for the general library collection.

Other Assessment Needs

Other parts of the collection also need to be assessed, including loaned or borrowed materials, rare books, fine art, valuable papers, and computer hardware and software.

Borrowed Materials

Every library borrows materials through interlibrary loan, and some items might be in the library at the time of a disaster. The responsibility for loaned or borrowed items should be clearly stated in the loan agreement. See ALA's Guidelines at www.ala.org/rusa/guidelines/interlibrary. If the borrowing library is responsible for these materials, they should be included in that library's risk quantification.

Special Collections

The special collections of local and rare materials should be separately inventoried and valued by item for materials valued over a set amount. There should be yearly updating of the collection's valuation based on donated materials and the auction prices for any similar rare books held in the collection. Property should always be identified with a specific or stated value for each item (or group of similar items).

Rare Books, Fine Art, and Valuable Papers

By their nature, these items present unique problems when trying to establish values. For example, precisely what constitutes a rare document? Generally, such items have an intrinsic value that is greater than the purchase price. This category might include original manuscripts, signed works, original maps, scientific documents, and documents that are no longer in print. Each library should determine the best value for itemizing each rare book, valuable papers, or other rare items. It is not unusual for a threshold to be used, depending on the nature of the collection. A typical value for itemizing is one in excess of $1,000 per title, though libraries with large collections may choose to set that figure higher. Yearly updating of values for rare materials is recommended to assure appropriate valuation.

Rare documents, once defined, should be inventoried to determine the size and nature of the items in the collection. One way to place a value on these items is to have them appraised, a costly process that is not often done, except for items of exceptionally high value. A professional in the field should price fine art, original sculptures, paintings, rare books, and similar materials that have no readily determinable market or replacement value. This professional may be a librarian for rare books, manuscripts, and other rare or irreplaceable library materials, and a local art dealer for original paintings, sculptures, and so on.

Short of an appraisal, the librarian can establish a value for these items. For letters and manuscripts by writers, as well as original music compositions, value can be established by reviewing auction values of similar writers or composers, or by citing the paid price and allowing for inflation every year thereafter.

It is important that these types of property are identified with a specific or stated value for each item (or group of similar items). In the case of irreplaceable materials, the loss of a single item could be substantial. Establishing the general condition of these materials, with a visual record of the condition of the most valuable materials where possible, is key to establishing the values at risk for these items.

Computer Hardware and Software

As with books, computers, software, and all EDP equipment are considered standard library contents. An up-to-date inventory of computer hardware and software is important for an effective valuation because libraries now rely on computers for access to many titles that are produced and made available electronically.

LIABILITY

It is easy to understand how physical damage to a library resulting from a fire or severe weather can cause a substantial loss of the library's assets. One can literally sift through the ashes or the storm debris and look at what once was. It is much more difficult to visualize the impact on assets from a liability claim. Yet the impact can be significant and, while unlikely, can even surpass the value of the physical structure of the library. One of the reasons why liability claims can be so expensive is that the costs to defend these claims can be costly. In addition, the reputational impact when there is a high-profile lawsuit needs to be managed carefully so as not to damage the library's standing within the community and with its donor relationships. Liability risks take many different forms.

The role of libraries in our communities has changed. No longer are libraries simply a place that houses books. Instead libraries have become vibrant hubs that support their communities in several different ways—they provide meeting places, have coffee shops, gift shops, special events, community outreach, rallying points in emergency response, and provide community emergency response shelters. With the increase of guests visiting library facilities for a variety of reasons, so too does the risk of possible liability arising out of guests injuring themselves. Libraries as public spaces, or community hubs, are not immune from lawsuits arising out of active shooter or other tragic events.

The virtual library provides additional scope for cyber liability exposures. The virtual library has potential liability with regard to copyright risks.

Employment practice liability risks around employee retaliation or discrimination may occur with any organization which employs people, and libraries are not immune from this type of liability risk.

Unlike in property claims where the actual damage or destruction of property is indisputable, in liability claims, it is the allegation of a wrongful act that leads to further investigation, defense costs, and judgment or settlement. For liability, libraries want to avoid the admission of liability. Where prudent liability claims may be settled, settlement occurs without an admission of liability. Depending on the nature of the claim, the settlement may also include confidentiality requirements.

Generally, liability claims arise from a civil wrong committed against another party. Such a civil wrong, or injury, is known as a tort. The courts generally recognize torts as compensable wrongs. Torts typically arise when a duty or obligation to another party is not fulfilled. For example, the library has a duty to provide a safe environment for those who use its facilities. Slippery floors, which could cause falls, or unsafe stacking of books, which could cause injuries, are both potential torts if someone is injured due to these unsafe conditions. (It is important to note that the duty or obligation cannot arise from a breach of contract, which has its own body of law.) A tort also may arise from the violation of a legal right that has been imposed by law. For example, library employees have the right to expect to work in an environment free of sexual discrimination or sexual harassment. Failure to provide such an environment may be deemed tortious conduct on the part of the library if an employee feels that these rights have been violated.

Public libraries are particularly vulnerable to constitutional liability risks. Libraries need to carefully review their policies on use and access, especially around use and access by political and religious groups. The virtual library provides additional scope for cyber liability exposures. The virtual library has potential liability with regard to copyright risks. Employment practice liability risks around employee retaliation or discrimination may occur with any organization which employs people, and libraries are not immune from this type of liability risk.

It is difficult to quantify the value of a claim that has not occurred or may never occur. There is no tangible and specific asset at risk. The liability that can result from a tort can vary from the cost of a damaged vehicle or lost book to the cost of long-term care for someone seriously injured in an accident. If the incident is considered to be particularly egregious, judges and juries can award punitive damages far beyond actual economic damages. Remember, as stated earlier, defense costs need to be factored into this analysis.

However, it is possible to make some judgments about the cost of a liability claim should the worst happen. In today's increasingly litigious environment, there are many examples of juries sympathetic to claimants recommending exceptionally large awards that are seemingly out of line with the wrongdoing leading to the claim.

In an assessment of such a potential liability, the library should consider:

- The litigious nature of the community it serves. Some states, counties, and cities have developed reputations as extremely liberal in awarding large judgments to plaintiffs. And even if the local jurisdiction has no such reputation, today almost no venue is considered immune to severe awards.
- The nature of claims and issues that have been successfully litigated against other libraries in the home state. The library should consider any current legal trends concerning libraries or their boards. Has the library had to cut its services to surrounding communities?

- Defense costs. These are dependent on the nature of the claim, the complexity, the number of expert witnesses that may be called, and the length of the trial.
- The nature of claims against business in general. Is there any civil unrest in the community that could result in actions against the library?
- The worst-case scenario. What are the one or two most catastrophic claims that could happen as a result of a tort? Imagine the worst that could happen and then increase the potential cost exponentially. For example, consider the possibility of an incident that could result in multiple deaths or long-term injuries stemming from a fire or building collapse due to the library's negligence in maintaining safe premises.

Once these issues have been considered, the library should be able to determine how to fund this worst-case scenario, generally though the purchase of insurance.

RISK ASSESSMENTS

The section on risk quantification and evaluation can assist the library in determining adequacy of insurance. This is essential for property insurance to ensure that contents are adequately described and valued, and for liability insurance to determine whether the insurance limits purchased are adequate given this potential exposure.

This section discusses risk assessments as a management tool, describes what it is, and explains how it can assist the library in making informed decisions. For example, a library is designing a new program to engage the community and increase patronage of the library. A risk assessment can help identify areas of risk and assist in the implementation of a new program. A risk assessment can also be used to assess a current program and determine where improvements can be made, or where additional resources or funding are needed.

What Is a Risk Assessment?

Risk assessment has several different definitions.

- "Risk assessment is a general term across many industries to determine the likelihood of loss on an asset, loan, or investment. Assessing risk is essential for determining how worthwhile an investment is and the best process(es) to mitigate risk" (Kenton 2020).

- "Risk assessment is the determination of [a] quantitative or qualitative estimate of risk related to a well-defined situation and a recognized threat (also called hazard). Quantitative risk assessment requires calculations of two components of risk (R): the magnitude of the potential loss (L), and the probability (p) that the loss will occur" (Stamatis 2019).
- "Risk assessment is the identification of hazards that could negatively impact an organization's ability to conduct business. These assessments help identify these inherent business risks and provide measures, processes, and controls to reduce the impact of these risks to business operations" (Rouse 2017).

Risk Assessment as a Management Tool

In the context of using risk assessment as a management tool for library operations, the above definitions contain the following common characteristics:

- Identify risks or hazards. For example, if a library is seeking to open a wood shop as part of a makerspace initiative, it should consider the risk of injury to participants in the use of power tools. There may also be other risks or hazards, such as an increase in fire risk (and damage to facilities).
- Not all risks or hazards are created equal. Some risks are low-probability but high-impact events. For impacts, consider human impact (the impact of bodily injury or death), asset impact (impacts to infrastructure or facilities), and mission impact (the impact to the mission of the library, which considers possible reputational impacts.) For example, the likelihood of death resulting from the use of power tools is less likely than, say, the risk of injury. But a fatality would have a significant impact on the library. This death example is what we would call a "low-probability but high-impact event."
- Identify either current strategies or possible future strategies that can manage or reduce the probability or impact of the event. For example, strategies to reduce the risk of injury from the use of power tools in the wood shop example discussed earlier would include the following measures: all participants are required to have a training and orientation session on the safe operation of equipment and tools, age requirements are strictly enforced, patrons sign waivers (release of liability) and assumption of risk forms, and library internal written policies are created for the operations of a wood shop.

- Implement the strategies. The library updates its written policies. The library opens the wood shop, holds orientations, training sessions, and demonstrations. Participants sign waivers (release of liability) and assumption of risk forms.
- Identify resources needed to successfully implement the chosen strategies. For example, will the library need to hire more staff, recruit more volunteers, or buy equipment?
- Identify the individual or team that will be responsible for the successful execution of the program plan.
- Always review the risk assessment process after implementation. Are the strategies to manage risks and optimize program objective and goals working or not?

The risk assessment steps described above can assist in the overall design of a new program, or they can assist in reviewing and improving current programs. Use any reported incidents, patron complaints, or losses as an opportunity to review the library's current practices and programs, and make the necessary changes.

Probability/Likelihood

The terms probability and likelihood refer to the probability of an event occurring. The discussions around probability tend to trip people up with some common mistakes or confusion as we relate our own personal experiences to the probability or likelihood of an event occurring. For example, we are more likely than not to ascribe higher levels of certainty to events that we have experienced, than ones we have not. And the converse is also true—we are more likely than not to ascribe a lower level of certainty to events we have never experienced.

Consider the following as a way of calibrating our thinking around probabilities:

- In a coin toss, there are two possible outcomes: heads or tails. Therefore, we would say that there is a 50 percent chance that the outcome would be heads and a 50 percent chance of the outcome being tails. But consider a coin toss of repeated events. After twenty coin tosses, we have twelve coin tosses that are heads, and eight coin tosses that are tails. What is the probability of tossing tails on the twenty-first coin toss?
- Answer: 50 percent
- Consider this statement: a "100-year flood event" actually means that in any given year there is a 1 percent chance of a flood occurring. In year one there is a 100-year flood event, and in year five

there is a 100-year flood event. What is the probability of a 100-year flood event occurring in year six?
- Answer: 1 percent

As in any human endeavor, our decision-making is not without risk. We may either under- or overestimate the risks.

Risk Scoring

In order to avoid some common mistakes around probabilities, many risk assessments simplify the scoring methodology by assigning numbers to qualifying words. For example, assign a "1" to negligible, 2 to rare, 3 to occasional, 4 to frequent, and 5 to always. Similarly, for impacts, risk-scoring templates will often assign 1 to negligible, 2 to low, 3 to medium, 4 to high, and 5 to extreme impacts.

It is always preferable to have decided on the risk-scoring method before the risk assessment begins. Clearly defining the method for risk scoring will ensure consistency and avoid confusion.

See appendix C "Risk Assessment Template" for a sample.

4
Loss Prevention

Once the library has identified risks and estimated the potential frequency and severity of loss exposures, the next step is to select the most appropriate risk management tool or combination of tools.

The basic risk management tools include avoidance, loss prevention and control, and risk financing. As discussed in chapter 1, risk avoidance involves avoiding identified risks wherever possible and feasible. As its name implies, risk avoidance is a very effective way of controlling risk. However, in many instances, this strategy is not practical if the library is to continue its mission of providing ongoing service to its constituents. Loss prevention and control, however, can be very effective and will be discussed at some length in this chapter.

Loss prevention and control are those activities designed to reduce both the frequency and severity of potential losses. They are activities that change the characteristics of risks to reduce the likelihood of loss or reduce the severity of those losses that do occur. Loss prevention and control activities include driver education, new employee orientation, supervisor training, early treatment of injuries, facility inspections, safety walks, inventory spot checks, and use of heat detectors, automatic sprinkler systems, and burglar alarms.

Loss prevention at the library covers a broad range of risks and activities. Because of the value of the library's collections, loss prevention for the collections will be the major focus of activities in this area. As a storage place for literature, knowledge, and often priceless materials, the collections are obviously extremely valuable assets to the library and its users. This chapter will focus on what can be done to prevent a disaster at the library and to minimize the extent of any losses that do occur.

The term fireproof is an anomaly when applied to a library building. Libraries' contents are combustible, and even the most fire-resistant structure will suffer heavy damage if a fire continues unchecked. Losses, no matter how well-insured a library is, are costly, time-consuming, and frustrating, and they divert resources, both human and economic, away from the library's mission of providing service to its patrons. It is advisable, therefore, that the library utilize all resources reasonably available to prevent loss. Libraries require a superior fire protection system for three key reasons: 1) the library is a central resource to its users; 2) some libraries have special collections comprised of irreplaceable items and materials of great value; and 3) the library has an obligation to provide safe premises and a safe working environment.

PROPERTY LOSS PREVENTION AND CONTROL

There are a number of opportunities for the library to minimize exposures: preplanning during construction of a new facility or during a major renovation of an existing building; installing physical protection, such as automatic sprinkler protection, smoke and heat detectors, and effective vertical and horizontal cutoffs; maintaining good housekeeping; maintaining and controlling ignition sources, such as smoking, electrical systems, and hot work; and preparing all hazards emergency response, disaster recovery, and business continuity plans.

NFPA Code 909: Code for the Protection of Cultural Resource Properties—Museums, Libraries, and Places of Worship, 2017 ed. is a good resource for libraries as it provides emergency operations, fire safety management, security plans, fire prevention, inspection, testing and maintenance of protection systems.

CONSTRUCTION

If the library has plans for a new building or an addition to the existing structure, it is necessary to review the geographic building codes and standards to confirm they are consistent with current design plans. Construction requirements would have been determined as part of the exposure analysis. In coastal areas or flood zones, for example, the building construction would take into consideration the propensity for flood and surface water damage. In earthquake zones, such as California, the Pacific Northwest, and the New Madrid areas, construction would address the potential for earthquakes. In the Northeast, for example, considerations would reflect concerns with the weight of ice and snow on roofs as well potential hurricane and wind exposures.

The library administrator should have access to the National Fire Codes and the standards and recommended practices prepared and published by the National Fire Protection Association (NFPA). (See appendix A for NFPA's contact information.) Specifically, NFPA Code 909 discusses general principles applying to library building construction, equipment and facilities, and fire protection equipment. It is worth noting the following statements from NFPA Code 909:

> The purpose of this code shall be to prescribe a comprehensive program, consistent with the mission of the organization, that protects cultural resource properties and their contents and collections from conditions or physical situations having the potential to cause damage or loss. (NFPA 2017, 1.2)

> Nothing in this document shall be intended to prevent the use of systems, methods, or devices of equivalent or superior quality, strength, fire resistance, effectiveness, durability and safety to those prescribed by this document. (NFPA 2017, 1.4.1)

Some insurance companies will provide assistance in reviewing construction plans and making recommendations regarding fire safety systems, which will help prevent losses. When new construction is planned, the library should make clear to its architects that loss prevention, particularly related to fire hazards, is a priority for the library. The library also should optimize the following design principles for fire protection:

- building construction and height
- types and location of windows
- locations and types of heating and cooling and storage facilities
- stairway design (such as whether stairways are open or enclosed)
- use of subdivisions to prevent fire spread
- fire control systems, including detection and suppression
- fire department access
- HVAC systems that control the spread of smoke in the event of fire

Consider landscaping as a fire mitigation strategy by providing fire-retardant landscaping. (Similarly, the landscaping should also consider flood mitigation.)

In addition, the building construction should address the means to prevent other loss exposures, such as the location of roof drains, HVAC lines, and water lines. Basement occupancies should be minimized because these often are exposed to flooding, water collection, or sewer backup, and they are difficult for firefighting. Floors should be sealed to prevent any water penetration—from sources such as sprinklers, fire hoses, water coolers, rest room facilities, and air conditioning—from passing between floors. Consideration also should be given to providing drains on each floor.

PHYSICAL PROTECTION

If fire and burglary losses are to be minimized, prompt responses by the fire and police departments are essential. Automatic alarms are effective for this purpose. Appendix B to the NFPA Code 909 provides examples of "Representative Fires in Libraries." It contains the following statement: "Damage has been directly proportional to the promptness of discovery, the transmission of an alarm, the availability of automatic fire suppression, and the concentration of combustibles in the fire area" (NFPA 2017,99, B.3.2). The value of the library's services to its constituents clearly justifies the expenditure for alarms.

There are a wide variety of approved fire alarm systems. These may consist of heat- or smoke-detection units or a combination of both. To be effective, a system should cover the entire building. Local bells or sirens should be provided to warn occupants of danger, and there should be a direct connection to the fire or police department or a central station. Burglar alarms are available in an even wider variety.

Of all the risks to which the library is exposed, fire presents the greatest likelihood of severe loss. For that reason, fire protection should be the library's primary consideration. Even a small fire can spread rapidly in a library given the concentration of combustible material there. In addition, the maze-like configuration of collection stacks in most libraries can make the evacuation of occupants difficult. A fire department's first priority is always the safe evacuation of a building's occupants, meaning that controlling and extinguishing the actual fire is typically placed on hold until the fire department is assured that all occupants are out of the structure. While saving the collection and building is vitally important, it will not be the first priority for the fire department if lives are at risk. As a result, smoke and heat detection, alarm systems, and automatic sprinklers provide the most effective and reliable fire protection for libraries and their collections.

Because of the high value of the library building and especially its contents, automatic sprinklers are the best form of protection in the event of a fire. It is relatively easy to freeze-dry and restore books damaged by water, but it is almost impossible to restore a book that has been damaged by fire. Automatic sprinklers will control and extinguish a small fire, preventing the spread of the fire to other areas. No other form of fire protection approaches the effectiveness of automatic sprinklers. There are several different types of systems: wet pipe, dry pipe, deluge, and pre-action systems.

- A wet pipe system is one in which water is constantly maintained within the sprinkler piping. When a sprinkler activates, this water is immediately discharged onto the fire.
- A dry pipe sprinkler system is one where the pipes are filled with pressurized air, rather than water. As one or more automatic sprinkler head is triggered, it opens, allowing the air in the piping to vent from that sprinkler and filling the piping with water. Each sprinkler operates independently. Dry pipe systems may be considered advantageous for the protection of valuable collections and other water-sensitive areas.
- A deluge fire protection system has unpressurized dry piping and open sprinkler heads. The system is directly connected to a water supply and when the system is activated, a deluge valve will release the water to all the open sprinkler heads. The valve is opened when activated by a heat or smoke detection system. Deluge fire sprinkler systems are generally used in industrial-type hazard areas that require water to be applied over a large hazard area during a fire emergency.
- Pre-action systems are designed for use in locations where accidental discharge is undesirable, especially with rare manuscripts or books. Pre-action systems are hybrids of wet, dry, or deluge systems.

One reason for the increasing acceptance of sprinkler systems is the fact that water from fire hoses causes more damage in larger areas than sprinklers do. Sprinklers pour water directly on the site of the fire, extinguishing it and reducing the necessity for higher volumes of water at greater pressures from fire department hoses. According to NFPA, "statistics indicate that for structure fires in buildings equipped with wet pipe sprinkler systems where sprinklers operated, 71 percent were controlled or extinguished with one sprinkler operating, 85 percent by two . . . , 90 percent by three . . . , and 93 percent by four . . . sprinklers operating" (NFPA 2017, 93, B.1.3.2).

Appendix L of NFPA Code 909 provides the results from tests conducted by FM Global Research. Those tests were conducted to answer the following questions: would fire be expected to spread in a bookstack; and if so, will automatic sprinklers keep the damage to a minimum? Two tests were made, and, in both cases, the answers were emphatically "yes."

For the first fire test, standard automatic sprinklers were installed over library bookstacks. In this test, one sprinkler opened in the second tier three minutes, forty-three seconds after the fire was lighted and one sprinkler opened in the first tier seven minutes, fifty-three seconds after the fire started. The sprinkler discharge stopped the spread of fire in the books almost immediately and gradually extinguished the fire. There was fire damage to books in 10 percent of the storage space of the stacks, and this damage would be repairable for practically all the books involved. Books in an additional 27 percent of the storage space of the test segment were wet to varying degrees, ranging from damp to soaked. All books involved would be repairable by drying. Heating caused by the fire deformed some shelf sections, but the structural members of the stack were unharmed except for paint damage.

In the second test, the same method of ignition was used to start a fire in unsprinklered stacks. A total of 89 percent of the books were charred deeply or completely destroyed, 2.5 percent were scorched, and the remaining 8.5 percent were soaked. Approximately 75 percent of the shelving was irreparably damaged. Some of the structural elements were visibly deformed, and others would not be safely reusable for live loads. These observations indicate that complete collapse of the structure was imminent when hose streams were applied.

Automatic sprinklers are generally effective only if water is available in adequate quantity at adequate pressure or if the library has its own on-site water supply. Therefore, installing automatic sprinkler protection also may require a water pump (commonly referred to as a fire pump) to provide adequate water for the sprinklers. Unless there is water available to the sprinkler system and the sprinkler control valve is open, the sprinkler system will not work. For this reason, complete loss prevention protection requires that sprinkler control valves remain open and be monitored on a regular basis. Chains and locks help keep sprinkler control valves in the wide-open position.

A sprinkler control valve in the fully closed or partially closed position is described as impaired protection. In this state, sprinklers might not be as effective as they are with their valves fully open. Typically, this impairment might occur when sprinkler valves are closed during renovation and repair work and then forgotten and left closed, or when a maintenance person tests for system leaks and only partially opens the valve. These situations restrict the necessary volume of water needed to control a fire. For this reason, contractors should never be allowed unsupervised access to the sprinkler valves; instead, a member of the library staff or the facilities management or maintenance staff should always operate the valves and keep a record of both when the valve is closed and when it is reopened. They also should ensure fire hazards are minimized during this time.

Until complete sprinkler protection can be provided, a practical combination of sprinklers and fire alarms can be designed so there are sprinklers in all high-hazard areas, especially those containing substantial combustible contents, such as workrooms and supply rooms. Heat- and smoke-detection devices with a central station connection should be provided in all other parts of the building, at least until fixed protection can be provided.

The library can minimize any interruption to the use of the library by carefully planning the installation of protection, such as water supply and sprinkler risers with floor valving. This could be followed by sprinkler installations on individual floors timed to the periods of least use. Feed mains could be installed next, followed by smaller piping. Considerations should be given to prefabricating as much pipe as possible.

GOOD HOUSEKEEPING, CONTROL OF IGNITION SOURCES

Assuming the library already has suitable construction, automatic sprinklers where needed, and an adequate water supply, good housekeeping practices and control of ignition sources are necessary steps to prevent and control property losses. The importance of good housekeeping cannot be overstated. It can minimize the causes of fire and decrease the likelihood of other property losses as well. Blocked doorways, halls, or exits can hinder firefighters or emergency personnel from responding promptly and properly in an emergency. This can result in a diminished ability to control and fight a fire, increased loss of library property, and possible injury to patrons and employees. Good housekeeping is a simple, yet effective, means for minimizing loss.

Enforcing no-smoking policies in all areas of the library greatly decreases the risk exposure from fire. Each lit cigarette represents a potential million-dollar fire loss. For that reason, the library should post no-smoking signs throughout the facility. The library should enforce these policies not only for employees and patrons, but also for contractors and other vendors on the library premises. This can be particularly important during construction because contractors typically work in areas containing large amounts of combustible material that do not have working fire alarms or sprinkler protection. While most libraries have no-smoking policies, policies may fail due to lack of enforcement or lack of consequences for noncompliance.

Regular maintenance of boilers, pressure vessels, and electrical equipment—such as the systematic testing and inspection of electrical equipment and installations to ensure reliable and safe operation—not only will prolong the life of the equipment, but will also help prevent major losses. Damaged electrical wiring, combustible material placed too close to electrical equipment, exposed live conductors located below baseboard heaters, and overloaded circuits, for example, all increase the likelihood of losses. To prevent these types of losses, the library should establish an electrical preventive maintenance program. Components of such a policy address such tasks as keeping electrical equipment clean, cool, and dry; keeping electrical and mechanical rooms free of combustible storage; controlling the use of portable heaters; using only qualified personnel for electrical work; and having electrical work inspected per codes.

Even if the library is fully protected by automatic sprinklers, the sprinklers will be effective only if the sprinkler-control valves remain open. Sprinkler-control valves should be chained and locked in the wide-open position. To be sure that automatic sprinkler systems work when needed, the library should ensure regular inspections are performed to verify valves are open. Again, this is particularly important during renovations, repairs, or construction, when maintenance personnel or contractors close valves and may not fully reopen them afterward.

The library should include inspections of sprinkler control valves as part of its regular fire safety inspections. Fire doors and fire extinguishers should be inspected monthly. Inspection records should be kept on file as evidence of good housekeeping practices.

A hot-work policy should be established and strictly enforced. Hot work is any temporary operation involving open flames or producing heat or sparks. This includes, but is not limited to, brazing, cutting, grinding, soldering, thawing pipe, and torch-applied roofing activities. A hot-work policy should require that alternative procedures be considered in lieu of hot work whenever possible. However, when hot work is necessary, it should be well controlled by a policy that defines roles for all involved, specifies clear authority, designates hot-work areas, provides fire watches, manages contractors, and conducts internal audits of how the policy is being implemented.

Appendix E "Property Loss Prevention Checklist," and appendix F "Library Safety Inspection Checklist" provide sample checklists.

PROTECTION FROM WEATHER AND OTHER
NATURAL CATASTROPHE-RELATED LOSSES

Assuming the library already enjoys suitable construction, good housekeeping practices, automatic sprinklers where needed, and an adequate water supply, the most basic measures the library can take to prevent weather-related losses are

- creating an emergency response team;
- routinely inspecting and maintaining the library buildings and systems;
- avoiding locating valuable collection materials in below-grade spaces and spaces that could flood;
- properly maintaining roofs and their drains;

- performing after event debriefs and reviewing all emergency response plans; and
- as part of emergency response drills, reviewing and practicing responses to events that occur at other facilities.

The emergency response team, comprised of people familiar with the library's facilities, is trained to react to emergencies resulting from specific weather conditions such as floods or windstorms. During all threatening weather events, this team would manage all loss prevention and control activities, such as

- turning off circuit breakers and power supplies;
- ensuring sprinklers valves are open and fire pumps are operating;
- notifying the fire department, if appropriate, or other emergency response personnel (such as law enforcement, medical, etc.);
- helping library personnel safely evacuate the premises or find suitable shelter;
- helping cover vulnerable materials, such as bookstacks, computers, office equipment, and catalogues, with plastic tarps; and
- helping with restoration (including freeze drying, mopping up water, and relocating wet or damaged materials).

HURRICANES AND WINDSTORMS

Additional steps that the library can take to minimize damage from severe storms include

- ensuring proper construction at the outset and paying close attention to building maintenance;
- regularly checking perimeter roof flashing to ensure it is securely fastened;
- making sure gravel is evenly dispersed over the roof; and
- moving water-sensitive equipment away from windows or covering them with plastic tarps.

FLOODS

Library facilities that are built within flood plains may have special flood mitigation measures. The 100-year or 500-year flood categories are misnomers. As mentioned in the section on risk assessments, a 100-year flood plain means there is a 1 percent annual chance of a flood. It does not mean that a flood is likely every 100 years. Similarly, a 500-year flood means that there is a 0.2 percent annual chance of a flood occurring in that area each year.

Water may penetrate structures through a variety of entry points—steam tunnels, buried utilities, sanitary and storm sewers, and buildings that are not structurally sound and capable of resisting hydraulic loads. Surface run off may be impacted by additional construction and changes in surface conditions. For example, the nearby construction of a parking lot may result in increased surface runoff loads that may exceed existing drainage loads.

The library can minimize loss due to flooding by

- maintaining and routinely testing sump pumps;
- moving most valuable collections, rare books, priceless artwork, important records, as well as high-value equipment and supplies, to a floor above the highest floor expected to flood; and
- performing periodic flood-mitigation studies. The purpose of these studies is to review existing conditions and identify possible flood-mitigation strategies.

WINTER STORMS

The library can minimize risk from winter storms by

- scheduling a winter inspection program and repairing significant areas of concern;
- ensuring roofs do not reach the maximum snow load before they are cleared;
- always keeping roof drains and downspouts clear and flowing, even if snow cannot be removed from the entire roof; and
- routinely checking heating systems and water tanks to prevent freezing, which often leads to burst pipes or the incapacitation of fire pumps and automatic sprinkler systems.

EARTHQUAKES

Steps the library can take to minimize earthquake damage include

- properly maintaining the bracing of sprinkler and other water and gas piping;
- installing and maintaining a seismic shut-off valve on the building's main gas line to prevent fire following an earthquake; and
- properly maintaining the bracing of book stacks.

Earthquake-actuated shut-off valves, unlike excess-flow valves, stop the flow of gas until it is safe to restart. They often are provided directly on small, flammable gas lines. In other designs, the flow of gas in a pipe can be stopped, or other processes shut down, by a signal sent from a separate seismic sensor to a control panel or valve.

For more information, see appendix G, "Contingency Planning for Natural Disasters."

ALL HAZARD EMERGENCY RESPONSE PLAN

It is important to consider and plan for possible emergencies and loss scenarios. Be informed of the type of disasters most common in your area. Hazards may include weather related hazards, such as floods, tornadoes, or snowstorms; fires; active shooter or pandemic hazards. Complete a self-assessment prior to finalizing these plans. See NFPA Code 909-49, Annex A, "Vulnerability Assessment Survey." See Federal Emergency Management Agency's (FEMA) website FEMA.gov for additional resources.

The library should develop a written all hazards emergency plan detailing areas of responsibility and those responsible for each area should work as a team. The emergency response team should hold regular meetings. Emergency evacuation drills should be performed regularly. Tabletop emergency response exercises are important in testing out emergency response plans.

The essential elements of an emergency response plan are to

- identify the goals and objectives of the emergency response plan;
- define what your emergency response team is expected to do in an emergency (evacuate, provide first aid, shelter in place, etc.);and
- identify any regulations covered by your plan.

An all hazards emergency response plan is a road map in the event of an emergency. It essentially explains the "what" while emergency management explains the "how." Emergency management has grown into a sophisticated discipline in response to devastating disasters such as Hurricane Katrina. Under FEMA's incident command system, it is a management framework designed to integrate planning, operations, logistics, and communications into a common, standardized framework.

An example of an emergency response team may include an emergency coordinator (planning), someone to notify the fire department (operations), a sprinkler-valve person (the individual assigned to check that the valves are open), and someone to call an ambulance or the police, if needed. In the event of a fire, salvage and recovery plans are required to protect the collection (finance). Such activities can include removing materials in an emergency, covering collection shelves, installing dehumidifiers, and freeze-drying wet books (logistics). If the event is large enough, someone should be identified as the point of contact to deal with all media communications.

The library may build rapport with a salvage and recovery company in advance of any loss by asking the company to visit the facility to conduct an educational survey. The company could make suggestions to the library staff about what to do in the immediate aftermath of the loss—one of the most critical time periods for restoration. The firm also can be on call for emergencies.

Once the emergency plan is developed, the library should test, update, and modify it as needed. A properly orchestrated action plan can do more to protect the people and contents than almost any other action the library can take.

FEMA's Emergency Response Plan Template
https://www.fema.gov/media-library-data/1388775706419-f977cdebbefcd545df
c7808c3e9385fc/Business_EmergencyResponsePlans_10pg_2014.pdf

BUSINESS CONTINUITY PLANS

Libraries face unique vulnerabilities when faced with major disruptions like natural disasters, health epidemics, or IT system failures. While emergency response plans protect life and secure facilities, business continuity planning allows a library to continue or rapidly resume mission critical functions.

Business impact analysis (BIA) attempts to predict the consequences of disruption of a business function and process. It gathers information needed to develop recovery strategies. The BIA is an important first step in developing the library's business continuity plan.

FEMA BIA worksheet
www.fema.gov/media-library-data/1388776348838-b548b013b1cfc61fa92f
c4332b615e05/Business_ImpactAnalysis_Worksheet_2014.pdf

Some brokers and insurance companies with whom the library does business may have personnel who specialize in BIA and can be a resource for the library.

Once the BIA is completed, incorporate its findings into the business continuity plan. The plan should

- define the scope, objectives, and assumptions of the plan,
- define roles and responsibilities,

- identify recovery time objectives for business processes and information technology,
- identify the recovery point objective for data restoration, and
- identify "how to cope" strategies. (These may include procedures, resource requirements, and logistics for the execution of recovery strategies, including relocations to alternative work sites, strategies and requirements for the recovery of information technology, and manual workarounds.)

Like emergency response plans, business continuity plans are all hazard (that is, they cover all anticipated hazards in one plan). Once a business continuity plan is complete, test the plan by way of tabletop exercises.

FEMA Business Continuity Plan Template
https://www.fema.gov/media-library-data/1389019980859-b64364cba1442b
96dc4f4ad675f552e4/Business_ContinuityPlan_2014.pdf

DISASTER RECOVERY PLANNING

Library employees use electronic mail and voice over internet protocol (VOIP) telephone systems to communicate. Libraries may have other IT applications that are used to support library business—from online catalogues and online loan and hold requests to applications used to support library financials and employee payroll.

An IT disaster recovery plan should be developed in conjunction with the business continuity plan. During the business impact analysis process, priorities and recovery time objectives for information technology should be developed. Recovery time objectives for an IT resource should match the recovery time objective of a particular library business function. IT recovery strategies may include vendor-supported recovery strategies and data backup plans.

PREVENTIVE ACTIVITIES

Online Catalogs

The business of the library is making information available, and the key to the business is the online catalog. No amount of insurance covering that information—and few protective devices—can equal the value of a duplicate copy of the catalog stored at another location. The online catalog is essential as proof of the loss sustained in a catastrophe, and it is equally useful as a guide to the library in replacing books and materials. Of course, access to the catalog is also essential to get up and running again, even if in a separate location.

For these reasons, preventing the loss of the online catalog is essential. The best loss prevention method is to make regular and frequent backups of information and to store them in a safe place. A safe location is one other than the library building, whether that is another building remote from the library, another branch, or a different library.

Computer Files

The proliferation of computer files and EDP equipment in libraries creates some special problems in protection. As the library increases its use of, and therefore its dependency on, EDP and computer equipment for storage of information, it increases its potential for catastrophic risk. But in most cases, information is also being stored on servers and providing that same information on a remote mirror server is the best means of protection. Duplicating the bulk of the library's records and maintaining updated duplicates at a detached location is the best loss prevention method available.

Computer Hardware and Software

As with books, computers and most software are considered standard library contents. The main computers or servers should be located in a well-isolated area without public access. The room itself should be of noncombustible construction, and the contents should exclude combustible materials, such as manuals, tape storage, and paper or plastic products. The room should be provided with central-station smoke detection and some form of physical protection, such as sprinklers. If a computer room is particularly critical to the library's operation, both forms of protection should be provided.

Digital image files also are standard fare in most libraries, either for access to specialized collections through the internet or on locally mounted files. In some cases, reserve collections (i.e., required reading for particular classwork) are electronically accessed. While remote access to materials via the internet is one solution used in the event of disaster, it is vitally important that locally mounted files are backed up and stored off-site. Moreover, a provision for the use of other computer servers in the event of a disaster is also important for libraries to offer necessary services with little interruption. Not only is an agreement for the use of these servers necessary, but also it's necessary to test the process to assure that files can be mounted on the equipment and run at the backup location. Testing to assure compatibility is critical.

Valuable Papers and Records

Valuable papers and records include records that have a value in excess of the actual, tangible value of the cost of their paper plus the cost of transcribing them. Many library records, such as historical, financial, personnel, and accounting records, may have an intangible value and be extremely costly to duplicate. In many cases, these records are duplicated electronically so they can be easily stored off-site. Maintaining a duplicate set of these records at an off-site location, and regularly updating and backing them up is a good solution to avoid the potential loss of these records.

Rare Books and Manuscripts

The library can minimize damage to rare materials by establishing a conservation service before any loss occurs. Because the majority of repairable property damage in a fire is caused by water, immediate attention to water damage can drastically reduce the cost of restoring materials to their pre-disaster condition. A visual record of the condition of most valuable materials can help determine the amount of conservation treatment required. For very old materials that may already have damage or considerable wear, it is difficult to determine the actual cost of conservation for a known incident without having first established the item's pre-disaster condition. If this precaution is not taken, disputes could result, impeding the chances for a quick settlement.

Outside Protection and Security

Even though police patrols may provide some protection against vandalism and break-ins, their efforts may be hindered by the design of the library building and the layout of the library grounds. The aesthetic value of beautiful landscaping and soft lights may have to be sacrificed in favor of clear spaces and spotlights to discourage prowlers and unauthorized entry. Arson by means of the book return is also an issue. Book returns need to be constructed in a way that precludes a fire in case someone stuffs the book return with combustibles or ignited materials.

Active Shooter Incidents

Active shooter incidents, whether in schools, libraries, or other places where people congregate are increasingly and tragically common. This is why emergency response planning must include active shooter training. The FBI defines an active shooter as "an individual actively engaged in killing or attempting to kill people in a populated area, and recent active shooter incidents have underscored the need for a coordinated response by law enforcement and others to save lives" (FBI n.d.).

It is important to work with specialists in the design and training of an organization's active shooter response, because the type of training recommended has undergone changes over the years and will continue to be updated as law enforcement and first responders learn from each new tragic occurrence. At the time of writing, examples include "ALICE" (Alert, Lockdown, Information, Counter, Evacuate) and "Run. Hide. Fight." Libraries should contact local law enforcement or the office of emergency management to learn how to arrange for active shooter training. For ALICE training, see www.alicetraining.com/resources/documents/, and see the FBI website's section on active shooter strategies and resources at www.fbi.gov/about/partnerships/office-of-partner-engagement/active-shooter-resources/responding-to-an-active-shooter-crisis-situation.

Protection from Theft

Theft of individual books and other library materials has reached serious proportions in some libraries. Several systems of sensitizing books and library materials are now available for use where personal supervision of the library's patrons and users is not practical. Marking materials with a property stamp even on rare and special collections materials is necessary to assure identification of stolen materials.

Please note that theft is not a covered loss under a traditional property policy. However, stand-alone fine art and special collections policies will cover theft. Fine art insurance policies are a great tool for insuring loss (also theft) of valuable and rare items.

With respect to rare and valuable collections, consider

- periodically spot checking the materials,
- separating high-value collections,
- monitoring access through key-card access,
- using video surveillance,
- conducting background checks,
- providing an orientation to researchers,
- observing researchers,
- requesting to see the photo identification or other positive identification of approved researchers, and
- reviewing all incidents involving security breaches and where appropriate making improvements.

For more information, see "ACRL/RBMS Guidelines Regarding Security and Theft in Special Collections," which includes information on marking. (The guidelines are available at http://www.ala.org/acrl/standards/security_theft.) This resource also provides recommendations for interlibrary and exhibition loans of special collection materials.

LOSS PREVENTION RESOURCES

Insurance Company Inspections

One of the criteria for choosing an insurance company should be its loss prevention inspection service capabilities and the competence of its staff in loss control and protection. An agreement should be reached with the insurance company for regular inspections and loss control services. The library's insurance company loss prevention engineering services may be particularly valuable when adding to a library, changing its configuration, or changing protection or detection.

Local Fire Department Inspections

Good rapport with the local fire chief is very desirable. The library should invite firefighters to become familiar with the layout of the library building and encourage periodic inspections by members of the fire department and the administrator or their designee. It is important to make sure the fire department is aware of and understands the fire protection system provided and has an effective preplan to respond to a fire.

FIDELITY AND CRIME

Any organization can suffer an employee dishonesty claim. The chances of a claim can be minimized by good accounting practices, including the proper division of responsibilities, such as signature authority for checks, deposit authority, and so on. The library's fidelity and crime insurance company can offer suggestions to minimize the chance of loss. An audit can identify potential control issues.

Social engineering fraud is where library employees and business partners acting in good faith comply with instructions sent via email to make a payment or deliver goods. A third-party fraudster who mimics legitimate correspondence can be very difficult to identify. This type of loss may not be covered in a traditional crime insurance policy, unless specifically endorsed with a social engineering fraud endorsement.

Loss prevention strategies to manage social engineering fraud risk include the following actions:

- Educate employees. Never send products or money to a new address or bank account without first verifying via a telephone call to a previously established valid contact at the original source to confirm that the request is legitimate.
- Establish procedures requiring two or more employees to sign off on any change to delivery or wire instructions.
- Document all confirmations in writing, and include the date and contact information of the employee.
- Regularly communicate with your vendors regarding any security issues with IT systems, including e-mail.

OSHA REQUIREMENTS

The Occupational Safety and Health Act (OSHA), adopted by the federal government in 1970, applies to all employees (except state and local government) with reference to employee injuries. Some states have taken over OSHA responsibilities from the federal government and may apply the regulations to state and local governmental bodies. The most important part of this statute for libraries concerns the maintenance of adequate records relating to on-the-job employee injuries. The details of this record-keeping requirement are contained in the U.S. Department of Labor booklet titled Record-Keeping Requirements under the Williams-Steiger Occupational Safety and Health Act of 1970. Specifics about record-keeping can be found at www.osha.gov/recordkeeping/index.html.

It is the authors' belief that most, if not all, libraries (along with educational facilities) are exempt from OSHA's record-keeping provisions, but not from the law itself. However, good management practice dictates that libraries should maintain internal records of claims, regardless of whether the OSHA requirement applies to them.

SOVEREIGN IMMUNITY

While sovereign immunity is not a true loss prevention technique; nevertheless, it is a loss control protection in the form of immunity available to many institutions. Immunity statutes assist certain libraries from dealing with the costs of dealing with expensive and frivolous lawsuits. Virtually all governmental bodies in the United States have some form of governmental immunity. These immunities vary greatly by state and jurisdiction and some have been eroded by court decisions that have weakened their effectiveness as a defense. Some immunity statutes will provide certain areas where a library is not immune from liability, but the liability limits are capped at set amounts for those types of liability. Liability statutes may also prescribe notice periods.

The administrator should be knowledgeable on the issue and inform liability insurers that such a defense exists. In some states, the existence of an insurance policy can be considered a waiver of the sovereign immunity defense unless an endorsement is attached to the policy stating that the policy does not constitute a waiver of the immunity. State statutes may also state that the existence of insurance is not a waiver of immunity.

The existence of immunity is not a license to ignore loss prevention and risk management best practices. Many immunity statutes do not allow immunity in cases of gross or willful negligence. Remember, public opinion can result in changes to state immunity statutes.

LOSS CONTROL FOR WORKERS' COMPENSATION

Repetitive Motion Injuries

While working in libraries are not inherently dangerous, there are patterns of claims that develop from library employees. Of course, any employee can suffer an injury resulting from a slip, trip, or fall. (Prevention is discussed in the section "General Liability" later in this chapter.) However, a pattern of claims common to libraries is repetitive motion injury. These injuries, if undetected, can result in serious damage and often lead to surgery and extensive rehabilitation.

Ergonomics is the science that seeks to minimize or eliminate exposure to the risk of injury by designing tools, equipment, workstations, and processes to meet the capabilities of humans. In workers' compensation, many injuries to employees are ergonomic related injuries. Examples include repetitive strains and injuries that occur when common movements are performed incorrectly, such as injuries from lifting objects or from prolonged awkward posture. Ergonomic control strategies such as evaluating workstations and job duties and educating employees on proper postures and techniques can greatly assist in reducing the severity of ergonomic-related musculoskeletal disorder injuries.

Repetitive motion injuries in libraries arise from two sources: shipping and receiving activities, and heavy keyboard activity. Shipping and receiving personnel generally handle, pack, and unpack books on a regular basis. The constant reaching associated with this process can lead to repetitive motion injuries in the wrists, arms, and shoulders. To minimize these injuries, the library should ensure the work is examined to determine how the ergonomics of the area can be improved. A visit from the company that provides workers' compensation insurance should be able to make recommendations to increase worker safety.

Keyboard-related repetitive motion injuries generally appear as a carpal tunnel injury. To minimize the potential for this injury, every workstation should have an ergonomic review. Most workstation furniture and keyboard equipment today have ergonomic features, but to be effective, the features must be used. Often, the equipment manufacturers offer suggestions on ergonomic structure. There also are websites that offer guidelines on the subject.

According to OSHA, in 2018 carpal tunnel syndrome injuries had an average direct cost of $30,882. Strain injuries had an average direct cost of $32,959. For additional information on the direct and indirect costs of injuries on organizations, see the relevant section of the OSHA website at www.osha .gov/dcsp/smallbusiness/safetypays/estimator. Ergonomic strategies that intervene promptly before an employee's discomfort reaches the level where a workers' compensation claim is filed can have real impacts on reducing costs.

Other Sources of Employee Injuries

Two other common types of employee injuries result from lifting or being struck by falling objects. There are many guidelines available for appropriate lifting techniques, which include wearing a lifting harness to support the employee's back. Finally, loose shelving has proven to be a source of employee injury, so all shelving should be anchored in position to prevent claims that result from unstable shelving.

It is important to review loss trends to determine areas where improvements can be made. Insurance brokers or risk management professionals can provide assistance in analyzing loss data. Factors to analyze include cause of injury, number of days a claim is open, total incurred costs, and number of lost days.

The longer a claim is open, the cost of the claim increases. Reducing the number of days that a claim is open will reduce these claim costs. The longer an employee is off work, the likelihood of the employee returning to work reduces significantly, resulting in increased claim costs in the form of indemnity payments (lost wages or disability payments) and delays in recovery.

There are some strategies that a library may implement to reduce the severity of workers' compensation claims. If possible, consider implementing a temporary modified duty program. This type of program offers temporary "light" duty to injured workers who are released back to work with physical restrictions imposed by workers' compensation medical providers. The modified duty must match that individual's physical restrictions. Any temporary modified duty program must comply with state workers' compensations statutes and regulations.

LIABILITY LOSS CONTROL

General Liability

Injuries to library patrons and the public generally fall into the slips, trips, and falls category. These injuries may occur in any location, from the parking lot to the aisles between the books to the freshly washed floors of the restrooms. Libraries, like all businesses open to the public, have an obligation to provide an environment that is as safe as possible from the potential for injury.

Parking lots should be well lit so that patrons can make their way safely after dark. Stairways, either internal or external, should similarly be well lit and have handrails for those patrons who need them. It is important after inclement weather to have parking lots and stairs cleared and dried as soon as possible. Aisles and traffic pathways should be kept clear of books, carts, and any other objects that can obstruct free access. Additionally, exit signs should be clearly visible and not blocked by shelving or other equipment.

Perform regularly scheduled safety walks of the facility and the parking area. Keep records of possible issues—such as possible trip hazards, poor lighting, and light replacement—and make sure any deficiencies identified are corrected and recorded.

If there are any incidents that may occur—such as a report from a patron falling on-site—record these incidents, take down the names of those involved, a description of what occurred, and the names of witnesses. Use these incident reports to identify possible issues and make corrections. Do this regardless of whether there were actual injuries, or whether a patron is seeking to claim from the library. Proactive loss prevention can assist in managing liability risk to the library.

Automobile Liability

All drivers should always practice courteous and safe driving habits. If the library has employment positions for which driving is a function of the job, it should review those persons' driving records annually by ordering a motor vehicle report. Drivers should understand that any major moving traffic violation, such as driving under the influence (commonly known as DUI or DWI) or reckless driving, may result in termination, even if these violations did not occur while conducting library business. If a library employs drivers, it is recommended that the library have a driver policy for the safe operation of its vehicles, and that all new and current employees are trained on that policy. The safe driver policy should clearly spell out the possible employment consequences that may occur if an employee does not follow safe driving practices, and it should set out minimum driver requirements. Auto liability insurance carriers and brokers may be able to provide templates for a safe driver policy. Minimum driver requirements may, for example, be that a driver may not have sustained more than two at-fault accidents in the past three years, any major violation in the past three years, or any combination of at-fault accidents and more than two minor violations in the past three years. The library may use a matrix as a guide for driver disqualification. An example is described below. (The library should always consult its own legal representatives when deciding on driver disqualification criteria.)

Example of Driver Safety Manual for Disqualification

The following criteria provides an example for safe driver manual as a guide in driver disqualifications. The Library reserves the right to deny use of a library vehicle to any individual.

Minor Violations (any violation other than a major violation)	Major Violations
• Violation of a motor vehicle equipment, load, or size requirement • Improper plates or failure to display license plates • Failure to sign or display registration • Failure to have driver's license in possession (if a valid license exists)	• Driving under the influence of alcohol/drugs • Failure to stop/report an accident • Reckless driving/speeding contest • Driving while impaired • Making a false accident report • Homicide, manslaughter, or assault arising out of the use of a vehicle • Driving while license is suspended/revoked • Careless driving • Attempting to elude a police officer

Drivers should periodically be asked to take safe driver training instruction. Such courses can be found through the National Safety Council (www .nsc.org).

Directors' and Officers' Liability

Though loss prevention in these areas is more intangible than that related to preventing physical loss, it is necessary and possible. The board should be provided with a manual that includes, but is not limited to, the mission and the ethics of the governing body or community, the board's responsibility to the community, and the administrative business rules of the library. New board members should complete a new member orientation setting out the scope of their responsibilities.

The Sarbanes-Oxley Act of 2002 was enacted by Congress in response to the corporate and accounting scandals of a number of companies, the most notorious being Enron. The statute, informally known as SOX, introduced new financial practices and corporate governance regulations, including the responsibilities of a corporation's board of directors and added criminal penalties for certain misconduct. The intent of this statute was to prohibit improper corporate governance. While SOX may not legally apply to a library, the intent of the act should be adopted.

Employment Practices Liability

Loss prevention strategies for employment practices risk include having appropriate policies that recognize and protect the rights of employees as spelled out by federal and state law. Employment policies must clearly spell out recruiting, hiring, employee discipline, corrective action, and termination procedures. The library should regularly review its employee handbook and its written employment policies and procedures.

Managers and supervisors should be trained accordingly, and employee issues requiring disciplinary action or termination must be specifically and appropriately documented. Insurance carriers and insurance brokers have resources for loss prevention strategies. The loss prevention guidance described below come from Chubb's Employment Practices Loss Prevention Guidelines: A Practical Guide from Chubb (www.chubb.com/us-en/_assets/doc/chubb-employment-practices-loss-prevention-guidelines_v1.pdf).

Recruitment and Hiring

All aspects of interviewing and recruitment are regulated by employment laws. Follow the loss prevention strategies below:

- Avoid questions that are not job related. Design the application and interview process so that applicants are asked only legitimately job-related questions. Avoid the appearance of unlawful discrimination by avoiding inquiries that may identify an applicant's age, gender, disability, membership in a minority group, or protected status under applicable laws.
- Establish or update job descriptions.
- Develop a policy regarding the acceptance and retention of applications.

- Require all applicants to complete an application form.
- Reference checks: Obtain the applicant's written consent before checking their references.
- Credit and background checks. This is governed by the Fair Credit Reporting Act (FCRA).
- Hiring decision. This decision should be made subject to the approval of more than one specified person.
- Offer letters should be in writing and should include the position, the start date, and the salary and benefits (in general terms). Offer letter templates should be reviewed by HR professionals or an attorney.
- Employment agreements should be reviewed by HR professionals or an attorney.

Workplace Harassment

An employer may be liable for harassment based on sexual orientation, gender, race, age, or disability. Follow the loss prevention strategies below:

- Have an anti-harassment policy. This policy should include a statement of zero tolerance—a description of conduct that constitutes harassment, a complaint procedure, a requirement that employer will investigate all complaints thoroughly and promptly, a statement regarding the confidential nature of the investigation, a no retaliation statement, and a statement that offenders will be subject to corrective action, up to and including termination.
- Ensure that the anti-harassment policy is distributed widely. Examples include in new employee orientations and in employee handbooks. Make the policy available electronically, and post it throughout the workplace.
- Periodically train employees about the policy. Attendance should be mandatory and should include the highest-level management employees.
- Managers must be trained that they cannot agree to keep complaints of workplace harassment confidential.

Individual states may have different statutory requirements. The authors recommend periodic review of current practices.

See Employment Practices Loss Prevention Guidelines: A Practical Guide from Chubb at www.chubb.com/US-EN/_Assets/doc/Chubb-Employment-Practices-Loss-Prevention-Guidelines_v1.pdf.

Fiduciary Liability

Insurance carriers and insurance brokers are invaluable sources for loss prevention and risk management best practices. The loss prevention guidance listed below comes from Chubb's Fiduciary Liability Loss Prevention, at https://fliphtml5.com/lnht/orxg/basic. Fiduciary loss prevention strategies include the following tactics:

- Selection: A fiduciary must be capable and willing to exercise independent judgment.
- Education: The orientation and onboarding of new fiduciaries is necessary.
- Thoughtful, informed decision-making is required. The best way to document this is to have regular meetings, a detailed agenda, and copies of meeting minutes.
- Oversight responsibilities: A fiduciary cannot abdicate its responsibilities to administrative support staff.
- Documentation and observance of formalities: Ensure that all meeting minutes, agendas, and deliberations are adequately documented.
- Conflicts of interest: In order to avoid fiduciary liability, ensure that all deliberations are transparent, so that fairness can be adequately documented. For example, ensure that alternatives are reviewed and reasons for a particular decision is clearly described.

Internal or external audits are a good way to independently check and review whether controls are adequate.

Employee Benefits Liability

Employee benefits liability most often is fiduciary in nature. Since that is the case see guidance above.

Cyber Liability

Insurance carriers and insurance brokers are good sources for cyber liability, breach response, and loss prevention strategies. Insurance policies often include ancillary services including webinars and protection services.

The administrator may be advised to involve the internal IT department or external IT experts. Great American Insurance Group recommends the following loss prevention strategies:

- Periodic assessments: Technical assessments include maintaining configuration management, maintaining software patch

management, following a regular schedule for applying patches to operating systems, specific software, and anti-virus updates.
- Systems testing: Ensure systems backups with periodic data restores.
- Perform security audits.
- Educate employees on the adequacy and security of passwords, the importance of antivirus updates, and so on.
- Create written security policies.
- Maintain a computer hardware and software asset inventory list.
- Classify data by its usage and sensitivity.
- Establish ownership of data.

5
Risk Financing

After identifying and quantifying the exposures that threaten the library's assets, and reducing the potential for losses through preventive measures—such as sprinkler systems, improved housekeeping practices, or preventive maintenance of key equipment—the library will still experience losses, albeit less frequently and with less severity than would be the case without implementing loss prevention measures. Therefore, it is still necessary for the library to have a financial plan so that it can continue to function and provide uninterrupted service to its constituents despite adverse situations. This step in the process is referred to as risk financing and is accomplished by

- non-insurance transfers,
- self-insurance, or
- purchase of commercial insurance.

NON-INSURANCE TRANSFERS

The primary purpose of a non-insurance transfer is to prevent the library from being responsible for losses that arise out of the operations of others with whom it does business. A library can use contracts to contractually transfer this risk to others. A non-insurance transfer is accomplished by an indemnity or a hold harmless clause in a contract or lease agreement. This transfer is an agreement whereby the third party with whom the library is contracting agrees to hold the library harmless from any and all claims that arise out of that party's operations. Because the third party has agreed to hold the library harmless, that party will then absorb the financial costs of any claim made against the library as a result of the third party's operations.

Where contracts have indemnity or hold harmless clauses, it is also quite common for these contracts to contain insurance required as part of the agreement. Contractual insurance requirements are a way to ensure that a contracting party, who is indemnifying the library, has the necessary risk-financing mechanisms to fund any and all claims that may arise out of that party's operations. In addition to insurance required as part of the contract, these contracts usually contain additional insured and waiver of subrogation provisions.

Waiver of subrogation provisions are common for workers' compensation coverage. A waiver of subrogation as part of a written contract prevents the workers' compensation insurance carrier of the third party from pursuing its rights of recovery against the library.

An additional insured contractual requirement provides that the library will enjoy similar benefits of being insured under an insurance policy held by the third party. Additional insured benefits are determined by insurance policy terms and conditions and may limit coverage.

For example, the library should use an indemnity clause in construction contracts whereby the contractor assumes all liability for accidents to workers and others arising from the construction. In the event a patron of the library is injured as a result of the construction, the contractor will assume responsibility for any financial loss the library may incur from this claim. The additional insured contractual requirement for the contractor's general liability policy provides a mechanism for the library to access the contractor's general liability policy. It is a way to provide financial backup to the indemnification clause.

The library would use the waiver of subrogation clause to prohibit the contractor's workers' compensation carrier from pursuing its right of recovery against the library for the costs of a workers' compensation claim of the contractor's employee who was injured on the job.

Contracts should be carefully reviewed to ensure that the contractual transfer of risk is well understood. Care should be taken not to accept limit of liability clauses. For example, contractual terms that limit a third party's liability to a set amount, or to the extent of insurance limits, should be treated with caution as they may have the unintended consequence of limiting the contractual transfer of risk.

Lease agreements are another area where the transfer of risk to another party may be the most appropriate risk-financing method. A lease relating to computer or photocopying equipment, for example, may be worded so that the manufacturer or owner of the equipment is responsible for the loss of or damage to the equipment, particularly if the manufacturer or owner is responsible for maintaining the equipment. However, it is more common for lease agreements to transfer the risk of loss or damage of the equipment to the library or lessee. Sometimes lease agreements request proof of insurance.

SELF-INSURANCE

Self-insurance is frequently confused with a lack of insurance in the event of a loss. But there is an important difference. A library that does not purchase insurance and then suffers an uninsured loss must find the funds to pay for that uninsured loss itself. The library may have to scramble in order to deal with the financial consequences of the uninsured loss. Depending on the size of the loss, this may involve a special budget appropriation, a bond issue, or the need to divert other resources to pay for the damages resulting from the loss.

Conversely, self-insurance is a risk management tool. It is a conscious decision to accept the financial consequences of certain risks once those risks have been identified and quantified. Self-insurance is usually accomplished through a budget-line item known as a self-insurance reserve. Funds will be allocated to the self-insurance reserve from each year's budget. The amount allocated each year will depend on the previously completed risk quantification process. Funds in the self-insurance reserve should be adequate to cover anticipated losses that the library has decided to retain rather than insure in keeping with the library's risk appetite as determined by the board (as discussed in chapter 1). In the case of large self-insured retention (SIR), it may be necessary to retain the services of an actuary or other consultant to advise the library regarding the appropriate amounts to be budgeted to the self-insurance reserve each year. These amounts can then be used to pay for claims that fall within insurance policy deductibles, and for claims for risks on which the library chooses to self-insure and not purchase insurance.

The library should self-insure those risks that

- are so small in amount as to present no financial hardship. (Examples include the loss of books in the possession of individual borrowers, damage to vehicles in the library's parking lot, and goodwill medical payments for small injuries due to slips and falls.)
- occur with high frequency and low severity or with reasonable certainty and predictability, so that the probable total annual

loss can be projected for budgeting purposes. (In such cases, the premium for insurance will probably exceed the predictable losses [for example, loss of books due to theft or vandalism]. In some instances, as in the case of automobile collision insurance, the library can reduce its premium cost by assuming a reasonable deductible or retention per loss.)

The library should insure all other risks that can be insured (that is, which are of an insurable nature). This will involve the design and purchase of an insurance program that will allow for the retention of small and predictable losses and the transfer of large losses that could have adverse financial consequences. The next chapter contains an extensive discussion of insurance coverage. However, before exploring the lines of insurance coverage, the library should become familiar with available professional assistance resources that aid in the selection of commercial insurance purchases and products.

PROFESSIONAL ASSISTANCE

The professional assistance the administrator needs in handling the insurance program may come from one or more of the sources described below.

Risk Manager

If the library is large or is part of a large institution (such as a university) or entity (such as a state or county), its risk management and insurance program may be administered by a professional risk manager. In these situations, administrators should consider themselves an integral part of the risk management process. While the system risk manager will usually make insurance decisions, the administrator should be familiar with the insurance policies purchased to protect the library's assets.

Consultant

An insurance consultant (either an individual or a firm that specializes in risk management and insurance consulting) may be engaged to assist in the risk management process, either in its entirety, or specifically related to the risk-financing part of the process. A consultant may be retained on a continuing basis to act on behalf of the library in the capacity of a professional risk manager. A consultant also may be engaged periodically to do specific projects, such as review insurance risks and lines of coverage, prepare specifications for bidding, or assist in loss settlements.

The primary need for an insurance consultant will occur when the library wants an independent and objective survey of its risks and lines of coverage, when it wants to request proposals for insurance brokerage services, or when it desires to secure proposals for its various lines of insurance coverage. Soliciting proposals, either for insurance brokerage services or for lines of coverage, may be made by directive of the board of trustees, at the discretion of the person in the library responsible for the insurance program, or, in some cases, by a statutory requirement for public entities to do so periodically. In any event, if the library does not have a professional risk manager, it may wish to tap the services of an insurance consultant for drafting specifications for brokerage services and making recommendations of insurance markets from which bids should be requested.

To prepare the specifications, the consultant must be thoroughly familiar with the operations of the library and with the risks to which it is subject. The consultant must be available to analyze proposals when they are received to determine whether they conform to the specifications and then submit a recommendation as to which proposal(s) should be accepted, along with supporting documentation as to the reasons for the recommendation.

Generally, proposals for insurance brokerage services and insurance coverage should be sought no more frequently than every three to five years, depending on several factors. These factors include the library's satisfaction with its current agent or broker and incumbent insurance companies, the capabilities of those providing risk management and insurance services to the library, and insurance market conditions. If the library is satisfied with the performance of the current agent or broker and insurance companies, barring a statutory requirement for bidding, there is no reason to upset those relationships. However, from time to time, it is worth entertaining some competition, if for no other reason than to know what other options might be available to the library. It should be noted that it usually will be difficult to persuade the better insurance markets to consider providing coverage if the library's programs are sent out to bid more frequently than every three to five years, or if the library changes insurers often.

The consultant will require a fee, which will be negotiated with the library. Depending on the services the library requires and the length of the engagement, the fee may be an annual retainer based on the actual time spent on the account or a project fee agreed upon by the library and the consultant.

Agent or Broker

Most libraries, especially those without a full-time risk manager, will work with an insurance agent or broker who will be charged with providing professional advice and service and placing the library's insurance.

Generally, the insurance agent represents the insurance company and the insurance broker represents the library. However, the agent who is in the category known as an independent agent represents many companies and will act on behalf of the insured, much like a broker. Only in certain limited instances, such as binding coverage, collecting premiums, and issuing policies or endorsements, will the individual be an agent of the insurance company; as a rule, these activities will not interfere with their role to act on behalf of the library.

A number of insurance companies operate with exclusive or captive agents, for example, agents who are not permitted to represent any other company. Such agents generally will not be able to operate in a legal relationship as agents of the library.

The broker or independent agent normally will have a number of companies from which they can secure premium quotations for the library's insurance program. If the library has not retained a consultant, a broker or agent will work with the library to draw up specifications and secure quotations from several insurance companies at regular intervals, usually, as noted above, every three to five years.

Occasionally, the library may subject the program or parts of the program (for example, only some of the lines of coverage or some policies) to competition from other brokers or agents. But the library administration should be mindful of the benefits of long-term relationships and stability in its insurance program. For this reason, incumbent agents, brokers, and insurers should only be replaced when there is a significant benefit to the library, either in terms of broader coverage, better service, or substantially lower costs. An insurance program should not be changed for a modest cost reduction unless there are other problems with the program, such as poor service or the questionable financial integrity of the agent, broker, or underwriter. As noted above, competition should typically be considered only every three to five years unless there are problems with the program or insurance market conditions that create a need for more frequent market competition.

The agent or broker will be compensated either by commissions or by fees. If by commission, the remuneration for the agent or broker will be included in the premium on the policies they issued or placed. Commissions are typically charged as a percentage of the premium based upon prevailing industry standards. The cost of consultation and professional advice provided by an agent or broker is typically included in the commission compensation structure. Some brokers also provide services on a fee basis, similar to consultants. In that case, the fee will be an amount agreed upon by the library and the agent or broker in the course of their negotiations. Note that the library always should request a report of the sum of all fees, commissions, and profit-sharing that an agent or broker receives on the library's account. For more information, see appendix H "Sample Request for Proposal—Insurance Brokerage Services."

Choosing a Consultant, Agent, or Broker

When selecting an insurance consultant, agent, or broker, the library should consider

- the reputation of the individual or firm in the community where the library is located;
- the individual or firm's relationship with insurance companies;
- the individual or firm's experience in working with libraries, museums, or other similar institutions and the individual or firm's experience in the field of public or private institutional insurance;
- the individual or firm's willingness and ability to allocate the personnel and the time necessary to complete the assignment in the time frame required by the library;
- depending on the library's needs, the specialized resources that the individual or firm can bring to bear for the benefit of the library; and
- the general competence and professional training of all individuals who will be working with the library on the assignment. This should include a consideration of the individuals' professional credentials in the risk management and insurance field, such as Chartered Property Casualty Underwriter (CPCU), Associate in Risk Management (ARM), Certified Risk Manager (CRM), Risk Management for Public Entities (RMPE), and Accredited Adviser in Insurance (AAI).

The true value of an insurance policy for the library is the promise of the underwriter to pay for a covered loss. At the time of loss, certain elements become critical. The insurance policies should be properly written, especially pertaining to the property or operations covered and the limit of liability. The name of the insured should be listed correctly. The insurance company must be financially sound, properly licensed, and of good reputation. Choosing a competent consultant, agent, or broker helps the library select an insurance underwriter that will satisfy these criteria.

Services Provided by a Consultant, Agent, or Broker

The consultant, agent, or broker will be engaged to assist the library administration in the performance of the risk management functions for the library.

Depending on the scope of the engagement, a consultant may be asked to provide any or all of the following services. Generally, an agent or broker will be expected to

- assist in risk identification and quantification, including developing values for insurance purposes;
- assist the library administration in its loss prevention efforts;
- analyze risks and review the insurance program periodically (at least annually);
- advise the library regarding appropriate deductibles or self-insurance retentions;
- keep the library apprised of developments in the insurance industry that may impact the library's insurance program;
- periodically test the insurance market to ensure that the best program is provided, including the broadest coverage at the best price;
- provide an insurance market comparison by comparing the limits purchased by other libraries of similar size and scope in order to determine what insurance limits are appropriate;
- assist in determining the best value to the library (the program with the lowest premium is not necessarily the best option);
- place and maintain insurance coverage in force with financially sound companies;
- advise the library administration of any changes in the financial integrity or business profile of the underwriters and insurance companies assigned to the library's insurance program;
- be available to consult on changes in operation and on new construction and their effect on the insurance program;
- advise the library on the minimum coverage and liability limits required of third-party contractors and vendors; and
- assist in reporting claims and adjusting losses.

Consultant, Agent, or Broker?

The argument is made that only a consultant on a fee basis will possess the objectivity necessary for a professional job. Conversely, the argument continues, an agent or broker compensated by commissions that are a percentage of the premium lacks the incentive to reduce premium costs because that would lower their own commissions. While this may be true in some rare cases, consultants, agents, and brokers are all professionals and, as such, their work should be judged based on the effectiveness of their services in assisting the library in managing risk and in obtaining comprehensive insurance programs at competitive costs.

There are means of measuring the effectiveness of an agent or broker just as there are of the consultant. Periodically having agents or brokers compete against each other for the library's insurance business will ensure the library has access to the most comprehensive program at the best cost. When this is done, it may be worthwhile to engage the services of a consultant to manage this process if the library does not have qualified staff or the time to complete the analysis necessary to make an informed decision. If the library feels obligated to place insurance with more than one insurance agent or broker, to either maintain competition or to reassure itself that it has the best program at the best price, it might engage a consultant to supervise the entire insurance program.

The Library's Involvement

No insurance consultant, agent, or broker can perform satisfactorily without the full and complete cooperation of the insured. It is essential that some individual who is thoroughly familiar with the library's operations and plans be available for consultation. Usually, this is the administrator or the chief fiscal officer.

The library board should review the risk management and insurance program annually, generally prior to policy expiration. In order to accomplish this, the insurance consultant, broker, or agent should arrange to meet with the administrator several months (120 to 180 days) prior to the expiration of insurance policies to review changes in the library's operations and exposures and to secure the necessary underwriting information such as payroll, square footage, real and personal property values, and auto schedule. Other types of underwriting information may include information on internal employee controls, hiring practices, and cybersecurity programs. The effectiveness of the insurance program depends on the completeness and accuracy of the information supplied by the library. The responsibility of the consultant, agent, or broker for reviewing insurance regularly cannot be met unless they have the full cooperation of both the library staff and the board of directors.

It is important to remember, however, that the library personnel responsible for this process are ultimately responsible for the decision and must make the time to be well-informed about the process and available options in order to make the appropriate choice. The library board and administration still have the ultimate responsibility for the protection of the library's assets; therefore, this responsibility cannot be delegated to a consultant, agent, or broker. In insurance, as in other areas of business and professional services, the quality of services the library receives will depend on the people it chooses to do business with and the library administration's management of those professionals.

Insurance Companies

After risks have been identified and quantified; loss prevention efforts implemented; risks transferred to others via hold harmless or indemnity agreements; self-insurance decisions made; and consultants, agents, and brokers selected, the library must make risk-financing decisions regarding commercial insurance. Obviously, the main offerings from commercial insurance companies are the insurance policies to protect the assets of the library from being lost, damaged, or impaired due to catastrophic occurrences. The next chapter deals with specifics regarding insurance coverage.

In conjunction with their insurance policies, insurance companies also offer other services that can supplement the library's own risk management efforts. Generally, these services are included in the premium charged; however, there may be some services that require an additional fee.

Initial Physical Inspections

Working with the library, insurance companies will develop a firsthand knowledge of the risks at the library by conducting on-site assessments of the library's exposures. The information gained will be used in the insurance company's underwriting; it also will supplement the library's own risk analysis and can help in identifying and quantifying exposures, so the library can evaluate the most effective risk-management techniques for the exposures identified.

Annual Inspection Program

The library should establish a regular inspection program for safety and fire protection purposes. Many insurance companies have loss prevention specialists who can provide engineering and inspection services to help the library develop necessary fire safety inspections. These inspections should help the library identify the vulnerabilities in its properties and operations, and then help the library develop plans to remove or resolve these issues to eliminate or decrease risks. (See appendix F "Library Safety Inspection Checklist.")

Recommendations

Especially with regard to the library's property, the insurance company can offer suggestions that, when implemented, may reduce the risks of loss of the library's most valuable assets—its collections and building. For example, the insurance company may suggest adding security for rare materials or suggest improvements to safety issues after a walk through.

Rating Agencies

There are a handful of rating agencies that analyze and publish opinions of insurance companies' financial strength and their ability to meet their obligations to policyholders. These opinions are generally offered in the form of ratings published on an annual basis. In the event that a company's financial status suddenly changes due to some unforeseen circumstance, such as a catastrophic insured event or a sudden increase in loss reserves, revised ratings may be issued. The ratings have a key that indicates both the size and the financial strength of the company. The oldest of the rating agencies are the A. M. Best Company and Standard & Poor's. The library's consultant, agent, or broker should help set a minimum standard rating for acceptable insurers, but generally not one less than A-minus. The consultant, agent, or broker should advise the library if the ratings should change due to unforeseen actions during the policy period.

6
Risk Financing—Insurance

Most libraries will buy the following types of insurance coverage:

- real and personal property, including EDP equipment, computers and software, library collections, fine art, rare books, and valuable papers
- boiler and machinery
- workers' compensation
- general liability
- automobile liability and physical damage
- umbrella or excess liability
- directors', trustees', and officers' liability
- employment practices liability
- public officials' liability
- crime and employee dishonesty
- fiduciary liability
- employee benefits liability
- cyber liability

For larger libraries and systems, each of the lines of coverage listed above is usually underwritten on a separate policy. The coverage may be underwritten by the same company under different policies or by different companies specializing in certain types of risk (such as property underwriters or casualty underwriters).

For a small or midsize library, one insurance company may insure the entire library, with the exception of coverage for fine art and special collections, which may be underwritten by specialty insurers. For smaller libraries, several of these coverage lines (property, general liability, and automobile liability) may be purchased together under what is known as a package policy. The package policy may include a variety of insurance coverages, depending on the underwriting practices of the particular company. In a package policy, the premium is the sum of the individual coverage premiums to which a package policy credit is applied. A package policy will generally provide a premium savings because the administrative costs are reduced for the insurance company if two or more lines of coverage are included. Larger libraries may still find, however, that separate policies written through different companies and different agents and brokers may sometimes be more economical and more desirable than a single package policy. Which option is better will depend on the insurance market as well as on what the insurance companies in a particular market are willing to underwrite and cover.

THE INSURANCE POLICY

Insurance policies, whether a package policy or several stand-alone policies for individual lines of coverage, are constructed the same way and have five major components.

Declarations

Policy declarations state basic information about the policy, such as

- the named insured and their mailing address;
- the name of the insurer;
- the policy number;
- the policy form or description of the type of coverage;
- the policy period;
- the amount of coverage;
- if it's a property policy, the locations, property, and operations covered;
- the "Line of Business" or "Coverage Description" may be listed;

- the policy premium;
- terrorism coverage;
- commissions;
- taxes, surcharges, and assessments;
- policy deductibles; and
- a list of forms and endorsements attached to the policy (which are numbered for ease of reference).

Insuring Agreements

In this section, the library will find information specific to the insurance to be provided, including

- coverage clauses that spell out what property, operations, and activities are covered;
- definitions of important terms used in the policy;
- definition of policy territory;
- explanation of how limits of coverage apply and how retentions or deductibles will apply;
- if a property policy, the valuation of the property covered;
- defense obligations of the insurance company; and
- for liability policies, the descriptions of when the insurance company is responsible for defense costs and when it is not.

Exclusions

This section, as its name implies, enumerates the property, operations, and activities that are not intended to be covered by the policy.

Policy Conditions

This section of the policy contains general conditions not related to the specifics of policy coverage, such as

- conditions that void coverage;
- the insured's duties in the event of a loss;
- requirements for filing proof of loss;
- other insurance clauses that spell out how the insurance will apply in the event that more than one policy applies to a loss covered under a particular policy;
- subrogation rights, which are the rights of the insurance company to pursue recovery from a third party for a covered claim;
- policy assignment rights;

- actions against the insurance company, which will describe the process should the library (insured) wish to sue the insurance company; and
- cancellation clause.

Endorsements

The insurance binder document usually contains a list of endorsements. That list can be compared (endorsements will contain a reference number or name) against the endorsements that are provided in the policy. Endorsements are important because this section of the policy contains any changes agreed to by the insured and the insurance company that amend the standard policy in ways that make the policy more tailored to the needs of a particular insured party.

To determine whether a particular property, operation, or activity is covered, the library should first review the insuring agreements to see if that property, operation, or activity is included in the coverage clauses. Next, it should check the exclusions to see if there are any listed that would be applicable to the operations that the library is insuring. Finally, the library should check the policy endorsements to see if either the insuring agreements or exclusions have been modified in any way that is applicable to the operations for which it is seeking coverage.

PROPERTY INSURANCE

In designing a property insurance program, it is important that the policy be broad enough to respond to claims for damage to all property owned, leased, or in the care, custody, and control of the insured. Further, it is important that the policy be broad enough to cover damage from a wide variety of perils. (Refer to chapter 2.) The property policy covering the library should cover all property and perils identified under "Property Insured" and "Covered Perils" sections later in this chapter. The amount of coverage should be sufficient to cover the property owned, leased, or in the care, custody, and control of the library. All locations owned by the library should be listed on the property policy. In addition, all locations that the library leases and that it is responsible for insuring should be listed.

Limits of Liability

Blanket Policy

Most library property coverage will be written to provide blanket coverage; that is, an insurance policy or policy form that covers more than one type of property and multiple locations in a single amount or limit of liability. For example, a blanket form covering library property may be written for a single amount of insurance and cover all buildings owned by the library as well as the contents of those buildings, including furniture and fixtures, equipment, books, library materials, and other tangible property. A blanket policy is desirable because it permits different types of properties at various locations to be included in a single policy with a single amount of insurance. This simplifies the administration of the library's property insurance program because all property owned by the library is covered by one policy with a blanket amount of insurance. The library does not have to worry that an individual piece of property is underinsured.

If the library submits an annual statement of values (SOV), most property underwriters will offer a blanket policy. The library's SOV should provide the underwriter with a list of all the buildings to be insured, and the best estimate of the replacement cost of each. Replacement cost is defined as the cost to rebuild the entire structure at current prices if it were totally destroyed. The library also should include an estimate of the replacement cost of the contents of the building. Again, this is what it would cost to replace the entire contents of the library at current prices if everything were destroyed in one loss.

Items need not be listed individually. Rather, an estimate of the total cost to replace all library contents is what is required. This includes both general and special collections. The replacement cost of the collections should be included with a list of the contents of each library building. (Refer to chapter 3 for a discussion on establishing the replacement cost of library collections.)

The library need only file an SOV annually, unless it makes significant changes, such as the acquisition of a new building or other property. The SOV is typically filed at the beginning of the policy period.

Some insurance policies will be written with what is known as coinsurance. A coinsurance clause requires that the values reported be equal to a certain percentage of the replacement cost, typically 80 percent, 90 percent, or 100 percent. In the event of a loss, the library and the insurance company would become coinsurers if the values reported are determined to be less than the required coinsurance percentage, an amount equal to the percentage that values were underreported. If, for example, a policy requires 100 percent coinsurance and, at the time of a loss, it is determined that the values are only equal to 90 percent of the full replacement cost values, the library will be a coinsurer for 10 percent of the loss. Whenever possible, it is recommended that reported values equal 100 percent of the replacement cost and coinsurance clauses be deleted by endorsement.

Even in a policy with blanket limits of liability, there are some lines of coverage that will be provided at a lower limit than the blanket limit. A number of coverage types will be underwritten with a lower limit, known as a sublimit. The most important of these coverage types for the library are fine art, valuable papers, and rare books. These are often insured on a separate policy underwritten by a company that specializes in providing coverage only for these types of collections. These items may, however, be included in the blanket property policy. In either case, the underwriter usually requires a list of individual items to be insured with a value assigned to each item. The value assigned may be an actual appraisal value, or it may be the librarian's estimate of the market value or replacement cost (if indeed the item could be replaced) of any particular piece in the collection.

Whatever value the librarian assigns will usually become the insured value, and the valuation clause of the policy will be written on what is known as a stated value or an agreed value. The wording for the insured value of these items may read "as per schedule on file with the company" (meaning the insurance company), "as per schedule submitted by the insured," or "as per schedule on file with the insured." Other lines of coverage that may be underwritten with a sublimit typically include property in transit, EDP media, accounts receivable, flood and surface water, earthquake, and terrorism.

When new buildings or new properties are added, the coverage may be handled in several different ways. Many blanket policies provide some period of automatic coverage for such properties. For example, the policy may provide that new properties acquired by the insured are automatically covered, subject to some limit of liability (a sublimit, usually less than the blanket policy limit) for a certain period of time (such as thirty or sixty days) even though they are not reported immediately to the insurance company. Before the time period for the automatic coverage has elapsed, the library must report the new property to the insurance company, along with information about the building, including its construction, protection, occupancy, exposure, and replacement cost. Some policies may require the library to submit all underwriting information regarding a new property before coverage will be bound by the underwriter. What is important is that the library knows the requirement under the policy.

Schedule Policy

Some policies, particularly for smaller libraries, may be written on a scheduled basis. In this policy form, each location owned by the library is listed and a value, or amount of insurance, is provided for each location based on the values submitted by the library. The potential pitfall of this approach is that if a location is insured for an amount that is less than its true replacement cost, the library's loss will be limited to the scheduled, or insured, limit of liability for that particular location. In a blanket policy, on the other hand, the total limit of liability is available for each location insured on the policy.

Deductibles

Deductibles are amounts, or parts of losses, that will be absorbed by the library in the event of a loss. Generally, the amount of a policy deductible varies with the size of the library and its budget and risk appetite. Because the deductible represents an amount of loss that the insurance company will not pay, premium credits are provided in return for the library's agreement to accept deductibles. The higher the deductible, the greater the premium credit the library will receive. A small library may readily accept a $1,000 or $2,500 deductible, especially if experience indicates that it is not likely to have more than one or two losses each year. Similarly, a larger library may consider absorbing a deductible that is multiple times those, and a very large system may be able to accept deductibles as high as $100,000 or more. Whether a higher deductible is desirable will depend on the financial position of the library, its past and expected loss experience, its risk appetite, and the amount of premium credit. Some insurance programs may have "retentions." A retention is like a deductible; it references the dollar threshold that is "retained," that is, paid for by the library before the insurance company's obligations to pay are met.

Cancellation Clause

Every policy contains a cancellation clause that allows either party to cancel the insurance contract with a certain amount of prior written notice to the other party. Most policies provide for thirty days' prior written notice by the insurance company. However, many insurance companies will agree to longer periods for prior notice of cancellation—sixty days' notice—if requested. The one exception is for nonpayment of premium. In this instance, most insurers reserve the right to cancel the policy with only ten days' notice.

If the insurance company cancels coverage, the premium earned will be a pro-rata amount of the annual premium based on the number of days that coverage was in effect. However, if the library requests cancellation, a short-rate penalty will apply. This means the premium paid will be more than would have been paid on a pro-rata basis.

Other Insurance Clause

Because the basic premise of insurance is that the insured should be made whole after a loss, but should not profit from a loss, every policy contains what is known as an "other insurance" clause. This clause determines how the policy will pay in the event there is more than one policy covering any property. In this way, the insured cannot collect from more than one insurance company such that the recovery will be more than the value of the insured property that was lost or damaged.

The other insurance clause will designate the coverage the insurance company will provide

- primary coverage—it will be the first one to pay in the event of a loss; or
- excess coverage—it will pay only after the limits of liability provided by any other policy have already been paid, and the insured has not yet been made whole for the lost property; or
- contributory coverage—it will pay based on a pro-rata share with other coverage in effect for the same property. In this case, each policy will pay based on the percentage its limit of liability bears to the total limit of liability purchased to cover the property that has been damaged or lost.

Property Insured

The property covered may include any or all of the following:

Real Property

- buildings, including all buildings owned or leased by the library, and those under construction
- permanently installed machinery and equipment
- landscaping

Personal Property

- furniture and fixtures
- supplies and materials
- books and library materials, including periodicals, manuscripts, films, prints, audio and video tapes, recordings, digital facsimiles, cameras, projection equipment, musical instruments and related and similar equipment, accessories, drawings, artwork, fine art, valuable papers and records (including library catalogs if the catalog is not electronic), rare books, and all other materials intended for the use of library patrons
- machinery and equipment, including computers
- EDP media (see further discussion below)
- accounts receivable
- improvements and betterments in buildings in which the library is a tenant

- property of others in the library's care, custody, or control, which includes the property of the library's employees (This category also may include a large variety of property, such as books on loan, office machines, copy machines, microform readers and printers, scanners, digital cameras, and other equipment. The responsibility of the library for these items should be clearly stated in the loan, lease agreement, or contract related to the equipment.)

For a more detailed description of real and personal property, please see chapter 2. Some of the property listed above may be excluded by the basic policy. However, it generally can be added to the list of covered property by endorsement. Other property (such as valuable papers and records and rare books) may be covered by the policy, but may be subject to more limited coverage both in terms of limits or amount of coverage provided, and causes of loss for which the property may be insured, which may be more limited than for other library property.

Property Excluded

Covered property usually does not include any of the following:

- accounts, bills, currency, deeds, evidences of debt
- animals
- excavations
- foundations
- land
- underground pipes, flues, or drains
- vehicles
- aircraft
- watercraft

Covered Perils

The policy may be written on either an all-risk or a named-peril basis. An all-risk policy insures the library against damage due to all risk of physical loss except those perils specifically excluded. A named-peril policy insures against losses from specifically listed perils. Most policies are written on an all-risk basis because it provides broader coverage for the library. When seeking competitive quotations from various insurers, the library should always include a request for a proposal on a property policy underwritten on an all-risk basis.

The following is a list of perils insured against by most property policies:

- fire and lightning
- riot or civil commotion

- explosion
- vehicle damage
- smoke
- hail
- damage to insured property due to aircraft
- wind (including hurricanes and tornadoes)
- vandalism and malicious mischief
- sprinkler leakage
- water damage from defective plumbing, heating, and air-conditioning systems
- collapse of buildings or structures
- glass breakage
- burglary, theft, robbery
- boiler and machinery
- property in transit

An all-risk policy will include many of the above perils. However, coverage for some perils, such as property in transit or glass breakage, may be subject to a sublimit that is lower than the policy limit. Further, it will exclude certain uninsurable perils, such as wear and tear, gradual deterioration, mechanical breakdown, inherent vice, loss due to dampness or dryness of atmosphere, changes in temperature, mold (unless it is the direct result of an insured peril), marring or scratching, and loss through the dishonesty of persons to whom the property is entrusted. In addition, the coverage will exclude certain catastrophes, among which are flood and surface water, earthquake, war, terrorism, and nuclear damage. In some instances, limited coverage may be available for some of these catastrophes, either through property policies or specialty policies (which are discussed below).

Flood

Flood insurance may not be available from the library's insurance company, especially for a facility located in a designated flood zone. For this reason, the federal government offers what is known as the National Flood Insurance Program (NFIP), which enables property owners in participating communities to purchase insurance protection against losses from flooding. Participation in the NFIP is based on an agreement between local communities and the federal government that states if a community will adopt and enforce a floodplain management ordinance to reduce the future flood risks to new construction in special flood hazard areas, the federal government will make flood insurance available in the community as a financial protection against flood losses.

The NFIP is administered by the Federal Emergency Management Agency (FEMA). The flood insurance policy is limited in amount and is not subject to endorsements or modifications. Coverage is provided for buildings and contents on an actual cash-value basis (i.e., the replacement cost less depreciation). Replacement cost coverage is not available. The maximum limit of liability available as of this writing is $500,000 per building for real property and $500,000 per building for contents. However, no coverage is provided for any property located in a basement other than building service equipment. A local insurance agent can determine whether the library's community is eligible and can quote rates and the premium under the program.

Given the limited amount of insurance available under the NFIP, libraries with greater values exposed to flooding may want to ask their property insurer if it would be willing to provide some additional flood coverage in excess of that provided by the NFIP. This coverage can usually be provided for an additional premium. In addition, libraries with greater values in flood zones should give serious consideration to placement of the most valuable parts of the collection on higher levels.

Earthquake/Earth Movement

Coverage for earth movement, which includes earthquakes, landslides, mudflows, earth sinking, earth rising or shifting, and volcanic eruptions, can be added to the policy. An additional premium will be charged for this coverage, which is typically subjected to a larger deductible than other lines of coverage on the policy.

Terrorism

The Terrorism Risk Insurance Act of 2002 (TRIA) as amended by the U.S. Congress periodically was passed to establish a temporary federal program to provide a system of shared public and private compensation for insured losses resulting from acts of terrorism. Property policies will typically offer TRIA coverage. The purchase of this coverage does require an additional premium. Please see the section on "Terrorism Insurance Coverage" at the end of this chapter for additional information about TRIA.

Additional Lines of Coverage

All policies exclude coverage for certain types of property and for loss by certain perils. The library may delete some exclusions by endorsement. However, there typically is a premium charge when exclusions are deleted because coverage is being added and a premium must be paid for any additional coverage. The insurance agent or consultant should review policy exclusions and limitations while considering the library's needs and discuss the available coverage extensions with the librarian, risk manager, or the business officer responsible for the purchase of insurance for the library. Some of the following additional lines of coverage are part of the basic property policy; others may not be included in the basic policy. However, they are important types of coverage and can be added to the policy by endorsement.

Debris Removal

As its name implies, this coverage pays to remove debris caused by a covered loss. This coverage is typically part of the basic property policy.

Demolition and Increased Cost of Construction (D&ICC)/Building Ordinance or Law

New construction and renovation typically must conform to local and state building codes. When a building is damaged as a result of a fire or other insured peril, a library built in accordance with building codes in effect at the time of the original construction may be required either to be demolished or to be rebuilt to conform to codes in effect at the time of the loss. D&ICC coverage, also known as building ordinance or law coverage, is available by endorsement to a property policy and will provide coverage for these situations. This endorsement provides coverage if the undamaged portion of the library is required by ordinance to be torn down. It also pays for the increased cost of reconstruction to make the damaged or undamaged portion of the building conform to the requirements of the building and zoning laws.

Temporary Removal of Property/Preservation of Property

Included as part of the basic property policy, the temporary removal of property coverage provides coverage for insured or covered property at premises other than the insured building if the property has been moved to a temporary location as a result of a loss at an insured location (in order to protect or preserve it from loss).

EDP Media, e-Resources, and the Digital Library

E-resources now account for a portion of libraries' total content. The implications in a traditional damage or destruction to a physical library facility are that access to the digital content would continue regardless of whether the physical library structure is accessible or not as long as access to computers and EDP is still available, and provided that the licensing agreements have made provisions for access to the materials in the event of disruption. However, digital content may become disrupted through computer virus or by a denial of service attacks.

EDP (electronic data processing) insurance covers damage to computers, media and data. The coverage and insurance evaluation for digital content will need to consider the various digital content licensing models. The valuation may depend on their actual cash value, replacement cost, or functional replacement cost. Functional replacement cost is the cost to replace an item with its useful equivalent. The data records evaluation method may include the cost of reproduction and the cost to replace or restore. Media valuations may include cost to replace media or data with the same kind or quality. EDP insurance may be included in property insurance coverages or may be purchased as a stand-alone coverage.

If data is damaged or destroyed, the valuation may include the cost to reinstall or reproduce it from duplicates. The terms and conditions of the licensing agreements for access to e-resources and other digital content may determine the extent to which a library's insurance policy would respond. Insurance policies generally will exclude coverage for property (in this case data) for which the library is not legally responsible. Insurance would also typically not cover the breach or cancellation of any licensing or access agreements for digital content.

Property in Transit or Property Off Premises

Property is generally covered at the locations described on the policy or within a certain distance of the insured property. If library property will be away from the premises, as in mobile units, or will be temporarily on loan in substantial amounts subject to a single loss, it is desirable to extend the policy. Some coverage can be provided for property in transit and at locations away from the insured premises. This coverage typically is underwritten with a sublimit, a limit of coverage less than the blanket policy limit. This will require an estimate of the total values at risk and may require a list of locations where the property is usually kept. Coverage will apply while the property is at a temporary location and during transit. Coverage for transit is usually limited to the United States. Therefore, if international transit is anticipated, it is important to ensure the policy is not limited to the United States, and, if it is, to determine the likely value of international shipments and request additional coverage as necessary.

Valuation in the Event of a Loss

Traditionally, the standard fire (property) policy was insured only to the extent of actual cash value (ACV) of the property. This meant property was insured for its replacement cost, less depreciation. Today, such coverage is rarely considered adequate. Instead, coverage typically is purchased on a replacement cost basis with no deduction for depreciation, as long as the property is replaced. The basic policy often still includes ACV valuation. However, replacement cost is typically included by endorsement. This usually will apply to all buildings and contents insured under the policy, including buildings, fixtures and equipment, and books and library materials. Books common to the typical public library collection are not available on the used book market to a significant extent. In the event of damage or destruction, replacement with new materials will be highly desirable. Such replacement will be at new, not used, prices, and replacement cost coverage will be required to adequately cover the loss.

When coverage is written on a replacement cost basis, a loss adjustment will be made on an ACV basis if the library decides not to repair or replace the property destroyed or damaged during the loss.

Some library buildings are designated as historic properties. If this is the case, it is important for the library to discuss the loss valuation clause in the policy with the insurance company. Where historic properties are the subject of the insurance, the policy should be endorsed to provide historic reproduction if that is required. This may require the library to have a recent appraisal, so the library and insurance company have an accurate idea of the value at risk, as well as an understanding before a loss as to what will be involved in restoring the property after a loss.

Special collections, fine art, valuable papers, and rare books, however, are usually not written on a replacement cost basis, but rather, are insured based on the stated value the library has included on the SOVs and provided to the insurance company (see below for further discussion).

Books and Library Materials

Two methods of insuring books and library materials are most commonly employed—blanket contents form and valuable papers form.

Blanket Contents Form

Under this coverage, books and library materials are treated as contents, together with furniture, fixtures, and equipment, and are insured under the blanket policy form as discussed previously. All insurance companies will insure books and library materials on a replacement cost basis subject to the standard limitation that replacement cost is not recoverable unless the property is actually replaced. If not replaced, the loss will be paid on an ACV (depreciated value) basis. Loss settlement is usually made based on the value of each individual book damaged or destroyed, although the adjuster and the library may agree to an average value per volume when a large number of volumes is involved.

Valuable Papers Form

This form may be used for the library's entire collection or for certain library materials that the library considers to be more valuable than those in its general collections. These are usually materials that are unique and cannot be replaced. Special collections may be insured as valuable papers. It is important to note that most property insurance forms limit loss recovery on written and printed records to the cost of the paper plus the cost of transcribing or copying the records when there is a duplicate available. Coverage under the valuable papers form is usually subject to the following conditions:

- It provides broad (all risk) coverage.
- It is not subject to a coinsurance clause.
- It reimburses the insured for the cost to research, replace, restore, or reconstruct records that are damaged or destroyed.
- It requires the insured to declare the unit values for various classes of property. (This restriction can be a serious limitation at the time of loss settlement if an appropriate amount of insurance has not been declared for each item.)

Either of the two forms should adequately cover the risks of loss. The blanket form allows for the greatest flexibility because the library is neither committed to, nor limited to, a specific value on each book or category of books, nor to a total value of all of its books and library materials. In a blanket policy, the policy limit of liability applies to the entire property value, building, and contents, including books and other library materials. In the valuable papers form, the amount of insurance applies only to books and library materials. If these are accurately valued, there is no disadvantage to using this form.

Rare Books, Fine Art, and Valuable Papers

Property in these categories should always be identified with a specific or stated value for each item (or group of similar items). Generally, such items have an intrinsic value that is greater than the purchase price. Rare books, valuable papers and records, and fine art are appropriately insured on a stated valued basis, that is, with a scheduled value for each item for which value will be the basis of the loss settlement. This basis may be in a separate policy or it may be an endorsement to a blanket or package policy.

The values may be the items' original cost, the value set by the librarian, or the value determined by a recognized appraiser. Rarely will the original cost of such items make the library whole in the event of a loss. In other words, the loss settlement on this basis will not be equal to the value of the asset the library has lost based on the current value of the asset. Short of an appraisal, another solution is for the librarian to establish a value for these items, submit the list to the underwriter, and establish an agreed value.

When an item is irreplaceable and there is no ready market for similar items, the value may be purely arbitrary and may depend on whether the proposed value is reasonable and how much premium the library is willing to pay for insurance. By insuring such items on a valued policy or agreed amount form, the insurance company accepts the stated value as the amount of loss if the item is stolen, damaged, or destroyed. It should be noted, however, that the agreed value or replacement cost is the measure of the loss only if the items cannot be restored.

By definition, rare literature is difficult, if not impossible, to replace. As such, in the event of a loss, replacement with a preestablished dollar amount will never fully replace the unique asset that has been destroyed. For this reason, it is critical to focus on protection rather than insurance for these library assets.

Time-Element Coverage

In addition to coverage for the direct damage to the library's property (building and contents), the property policy can be endorsed to provide coverage for what is known as consequential loss, or the loss resulting from damage to the insured's property. Damage or destruction of the library's facilities can disrupt revenue flow, cause a direct loss of income, or increase its operating costs. The intent of time-element insurance is to place the library in the same position it would have been in had no loss occurred. The term time element refers to losses incurred due to the passage of time. The major lines of time-element coverage for a library to consider include the following:

- Business interruption, which covers the loss of income sustained as a result of a covered loss and provides coverage for continuing fixed expenses incurred by the library during the period of restoration. The loss of income could include the sales of used books and cafeteria or coffee shop sales, for example. Covered continued expenses may include salaries, employee benefits, and lease or rent payments.
- Extra expense, which covers those additional costs, over and above normal operating costs, that are necessary to reestablish normal operations after a loss. Examples include overtime for non-exempt staff, expedited delivery of equipment, additional costs for interlibrary loans, and the rental of EDP equipment.
- Expediting expense, which provides for the extra cost incurred on either temporary repairs or overtime labor costs, and the cost to expedite permanent repairs.

- Rental income, which provides coverage for the rental fees that the library is unable to collect from a tenant in a building owned by the library due to a loss from an insured peril.
- Leasehold interest, which provides coverage for the library in the event the premises it leases are damaged due to a covered peril and the library must rent other space at an increased cost. Leasehold interest insurance provides coverage for the additional rent the library must pay at the new location.

Boiler and Machinery Coverage

Boilers, machinery, and other equipment may be covered by the property policy. However, in the event they are excluded, a separate boiler and machinery (B&M) policy may be required. B&M insurance provides coverage for mechanical, electrical, or pressure failure of any equipment that is not excluded. B&M insurance covers boilers, pressure vessels, refrigerating systems, engines, turbines, air tanks, furnaces, generators, motors, and cogeneration plants.

The insurance company provides professional inspection services required by state law. These inspections fulfill a twofold purpose. First, inspectors are licensed by the state (or municipality), and their inspections satisfy the inspection requirements of the state or municipal code. In some instances, it may be required—in other instances, it is desirable—to insure hot-water boilers (even though a hot-water boiler explosion is not excluded under the property policy). The insurance company's inspection can be used to satisfy the governmental inspection requirements for this type of heating plant. Second, these inspectors are trained engineers. In addition to satisfying the legal requirements for inspections, they assist in the library's loss prevention efforts by inspecting boilers, machinery, and other equipment to search for evidence of faulty conditions or mechanical weakness. This enables the library to fix potentially dangerous situations before a loss occurs.

Comprehensive B&M coverage is available on a replacement cost basis. The policy covers equipment breakdowns and provides property damage coverage (for loss to the damaged boilers or other equipment), business interruption, extra expense, and other consequential damages resulting from the loss to the boiler, machinery, or other equipment.

Property Insurance Rates

Rates for commercial, industrial, and public buildings are based on those buildings' individual features of construction, occupancy, protection, and exposure—known in the insurance industry as COPE factors. Insurance rates vary from one insurance company to the next and may be adjusted by the insurance company following a personal inspection of each building prior to binding coverage. The library often can obtain reduced rates by making improvements in construction, physical protection, and by other loss-prevention efforts (as described in chapter 4). In most cases, insurance companies have some flexibility in rating. Where the premium is substantial, the library's actual loss experience will be important and may be a factor in establishing property rates.

CRIME/EMPLOYEE DISHONESTY

Crime coverage may be purchased either under a comprehensive crime policy or as individual coverage in the event the library does not feel the need for a comprehensive crime policy. Smaller libraries that purchase a package policy that includes property, liability, and boiler and machinery coverage also may include crime coverage. A comprehensive crime policy may include coverage for the situations discussed in the sections below.

Employee Dishonesty

This insurance protects the library against loss resulting from the dishonesty of library employees. Loss of money, securities, or other property as a result of fraud, forgery, embezzlement, or theft is covered. As noted above, this coverage may be purchased separately if there is no need for the additional crime coverage. This coverage, also known as fidelity bond insurance, may be purchased on a blanket basis, which is most common. In this case, coverage is provided for all library employees (all employees are bonded). Library volunteers who handle money also may be included in a blanket bond. Or the coverage may be purchased on a more limited basis either to cover specific individuals or specific positions, such as a treasurer or controller. The Employee Retirement Income and Securities Act (ERISA) requires trustees of the library's pension plans be covered by a fidelity bond.

Theft, Disappearance, and Destruction

This coverage protects the library against the loss of money and securities both on and off library premises, such as while in the custody of a messenger service. Some coverage for money and securities is usually included in the property policy. However, this coverage is typically subject to a sublimit, and the additional coverage provided by a comprehensive crime policy may be needed to provide adequate limits of liability, especially for a large library.

Money Orders and Counterfeit Money

This coverage will cover the library for loss directly caused by the library's good faith acceptance of counterfeit money or money orders.

Depositor's Forgery

This insurance protects the library in the event checks or drafts drawn on the library's account are forged or altered by employees or others.

Computer Fraud

This coverage protects the library from the loss of money, securities, and other property due to the theft of that property directly related to the use of any computer to fraudulently cause a transfer of that property from inside the premises to a person other than a messenger outside the premises or to a place outside those premises.

Social Engineering Fraud

This coverage protects the library when employees or business partners, acting in good faith, comply with instructions sent via e-mail to make fraudulent payment or deliver goods to a party who has not legitimately purchased them. This type of loss is often not covered in a property policy that includes crime coverage or in a stand-alone crime policy, unless specifically endorsed.

LIABILITY

Liability insurance is intended to protect the insured against claims for injuries to persons or to property owned by someone other than the library arising out of the negligence of the library and/or its employees. Generally, it applies to the unintentional tort of negligence, although coverage also is available where the act is intentional, but the injury unintended. An important reason for a library to purchase liability insurance is to provide a means to fund defense costs against lawsuits, which are covered by the insurer under this type of policy.

General Liability

While there is a standardized commercial general liability policy form published by the Insurance Service Office (ISO), there are many variations of this form in use by insurance companies. The discussions following are, therefore, only general descriptions of the coverage typically included in these types of policies. The risk management consultant, broker, or agent will advise the library on the specifics of coverage upon placing the coverage with an insurer.

Liability insurance is intended to protect the insured against claims for injuries to persons or property owned by someone other than the library arising out of negligence of the library and/or its employees. Generally, it applies to the unintentional tort of negligence, although coverage also is available where the act is intentional, but the injury unintended. An important reason for a library to purchase liability insurance is to provide a means to fund defense costs, which are covered by the insurer under this type of policy.

Bodily Injury (BI)

This coverage is intended to apply to injuries to third persons arising as a result of the negligence of the library, its employees, or agents. The term bodily injury includes death. (Employee injuries fall within workers' compensation statutes and policies.)

Personal Injury (PI)

A broader term than bodily injury, personal injury includes certain additional torts that are listed in the standard liability forms as follows:

- false arrest, detention or imprisonment, or malicious prosecution
- libel, slander, defamation, or violation of right of privacy
- wrongful entry, eviction, or other invasion of right of privacy

The standard personal injury endorsement excludes coverage for claims made against the library by its employees. (This coverage is discussed later in this chapter, in the section "Employment Practices Liability.") Personal injury coverage can be purchased as an endorsement to the directors' and officers' liability policy.

Property Damage (PD)

This refers to the library's liability for damage to property of others caused by the negligence of the library, its employees, or agents. This is especially important if the library building is located in a congested area and where a negligent fire or explosion might damage neighboring property. The standard liability policy does not cover liability for damage to property in the care, custody, or control of (also known as CCC), or used or occupied by, the insured. For an additional premium, this exclusion may be eliminated, or this coverage may be available under the property policy.

Comprehensive General Liability (CGL)

This coverage may be contained in a separate policy or as part of a package policy. It will include both bodily injury and property damage liability for occurrences arising out of library activities, including ownership and occupancy of premises, operations, elevator liability, independent contractors, personal injury, and products liability.

The suggested limits of liability will vary according to the geographic location, population concentration, library size, and business practices in the community. Due to changes in the legal climate, the limits of liability should be periodically reviewed because limits considered reasonable in the past may no longer be sufficient. When reviewing limits of liability, consider comparing what other libraries of similar size and scope are purchasing. The minimum limits the library should protect itself with are a $1 million combined single limit of liability for bodily injury and property damage, although some libraries may be prevented by statute from buying above certain limits.

The standard CGL policy protects the library as well as individual directors, trustees, officers, and employees acting within the course and scope of their employment. Such coverage is important because, in most liability claims that are based on negligence, the individual employee who committed the negligent act may be equally liable with the employer. Additionally, the employer may by liable under the legal principle of respondeat superior, which is a legal doctrine that assigns liability to another. For example, the employer, for the negligent acts of its employees acting within the course and scope of their employment. Employees normally do not have insurance under their personal insurance policies for business risks; therefore, they should be covered by the library's policy. The policy will contain a description of who is covered in the definition section of the document. This definition will typically include the employees, agents, and volunteers of the insured.

It is common for general liability policies to include "medical payments" coverage. This is a useful coverage because it provides coverage that reimburses others, such as library patrons, visitors, or volunteers, without regard for the library's liability, for medical expenses incurred on the library's premises. The policy will describe the conditions for coverage. Usually coverage is limited to a set dollar amount, considerably lower than the policy limit, for example, $10,000. There may be other conditions described in the policy.

Most general liability policies provide blanket contractual liability that will cover all contractual liability assumed by the library. Indemnity agreements in leases, sidewalk permits, easements, and elevator maintenance agreements will be automatically insured under a standard liability policy. However, care should be taken not to assume that all contractual obligations are covered by a liability policy. Careful review of the definition of contractual liability contained in the policy will demonstrate that this coverage does not cover the library from contractual breach of contract. The contractual liability coverage typically includes limiting language, such as limiting the contractual liability to cases where there is an underlying tort.

Products liability applies to the liability that might arise out of an injury caused by a product distributed to members of the public. This has relatively little application to a library's normal operations, but it could involve a risk when food is dispensed in the library and is consumed off the premises, resulting in injury. The premium charge for the coverage is nominal.

Dram shop, also known as liquor law legal liability, may be a necessity in certain instances. Some state statutes provide that anyone injured by an intoxicated person shall have a direct action against the one who served liquor to such person. The statutes may apply to hosts, such as one serving customers, employees, or benefactors. Host liquor liability coverage is generally available in these situations at a modest cost and should be considered by libraries serving liquor at meetings or receptions.

Coverage for the property of others should be obtained in some cases. The property damage portion of the general liability policy excludes liability for damage to property rented to, used by, or in the care, custody, or control of the insured. Fire legal liability coverage is intended to cover the catastrophe risk of liability for fire damage to a building that a library leases from another. The risk arises when an owner or its insurer (through subrogation) makes a claim against the library for an allegedly negligent fire.

Defense Costs

The policy will define whether the limits of liability purchased include defense costs, or whether defense costs are in excess of the policy's limits. The value of liability insurance is to protect the library's financial resources. Where defense costs are included in the limits purchased, consider purchasing increased limits. The value of a liability policy is not worth much if it is exhausted when you really need it.

Occurrence or Claims-Made Policies

The policy will describe whether the liability policy is occurrence based or whether it is a claims-made policy. Occurrence based liability policies are insurance policies that will respond where they are in existence at the time of the alleged wrongful or negligent act or occurrence. For example, the library purchases an occurrence based liability policy for the period July 1, 2017 to July 1, 2018. On August 15, 2018, the library receives a claim from a guest who broke their ankle on the library's premises on March 15, 2018, alleging that the library is negligent and claiming $150,000 from the library. The policy in existence at the time of the occurrence is the policy with the policy term July 1, 2017–July 1, 2018. It would be that policy that would respond to this claim since it is an occurrence based policy and it was in effect at the time of the alleged negligence.

A claims-made policy will only respond to claims made within its policy term. For example, if the library has purchased a claims-made policy with an effective date of July 1, 2019, and if a claim is made June 30, 2019, the policy would not respond because the claim was made prior to the effective date of that insurance policy.

Policy Exclusions

Liability policies will typically exclude coverage for

- workers' compensation,
- crime coverage,
- errors and omissions, and
- environmental exposures.

Liability Insurance Rates

A liability premium is based on number of patrons, amount of operating budget, geographic locale, and scope and nature of library operations. In most cases, insurance companies have some flexibility in rating and, where premium is substantial, actual loss experience of the library will be important.

AUTOMOBILE INSURANCE

Auto Liability

Owned vehicles licensed for highway use are required by law in most, if not all states, to be insured for bodily injury and property damage liability. Minimum liability limits are set by the individual states. However, in most instances, the library should strongly consider purchasing coverage with limits at least as high as those recommended above for general liability; namely, a $1 million combined single limit of liability for bodily injury and property damage. The standard auto policy covers the library as well as anyone for whom the library is acting and any person driving library vehicles with the library's permission.

Physical Damage Insurance

Generally known as "comprehensive fire and theft and collision coverage," this coverage should be included in all policies. For ordinary vehicles, a $250, $500, $1,000, or even higher deductible for collision is standard. For expensive units such as a bookmobile, a higher deductible should be considered and may even be required by underwriters. A large library or institution with a fleet of vehicles may be justified in accepting a higher deductible or even self-insuring all physical damage, except for the catastrophe risk of fire or similar damage, if many vehicles are stored at a single location.

Non-owned Auto Liability

The library is subject to this additional risk. Under the legal doctrine of respondeat superior, an employer is responsible for the torts of its employees committed in the course of their duties. This means that a staff member who is sent to the hardware store by the librarian—and drives their own car—will incur a liability on behalf of the library if an accident occurs. This applies even though the employee may be prohibited by library rules from driving a privately owned car. If the employee has auto liability insurance, the library will be covered under the employee's policy. However, the employee may have inadequate or no insurance. Some personal auto liability policies may have a "business pursuits" exclusion. To protect itself against such a contingency, the library needs non-ownership coverage. This can include liability for all non-owned and hired cars. It is important for library employees to understand that this coverage will be in excess of the employee's own personal automobile insurance.

If the library owns licensed vehicles, a comprehensive automobile liability and physical damage policy will cover all the aforementioned exposures to risk. If it owns no vehicles, the auto non-ownership risk will usually be added by endorsement to the general liability or the package policy.

Automobile Insurance Rates

The automobile liability and physical damage premium is based on the number of vehicles, kinds of vehicles, their garaging location, and use. In most cases, insurance companies have some flexibility in rating and, where the premium is substantial, the actual loss experience of the library will be important.

UMBRELLA (EXCESS) LIABILITY

Umbrella liability coverage is written as a separate policy to apply as excess over the primary liability policies (general liability and auto liability) in multiples of $5 million. For small public libraries, it may be possible for the municipality to list the library as an additional insured on its policy for a nominal premium. Limits greater than $5 million are not uncommon for public properties or where large groups may be assembled. Institutional risks are now purchasing even higher limits. Even a small library with an annual budget of less than $200 million may want to consider purchasing umbrella (excess) insurance with limits of $50 million, or by establishing a ratio of budget to insurance limits.

Usually, the umbrella policy will be broader than the underlying (or primary) general liability and auto liability policies. Claims that come under the umbrella, but that are not covered by the primary policies, are subject to a self-insured retention or deductible that may vary.

WORKERS' COMPENSATION AND EMPLOYER'S LIABILITY

Public bodies, including libraries, usually are subject to the Workers' Compensation Act and should be covered by workers' compensation insurance. The individual state law should be consulted in this regard. In any event, the insurance provides indemnity for the injured employee and protection for the library.

State statutes create a liability on the part of an employer for medical expenses and lost wages that an employee incurs as a result of a work-related injury or illness. The employer is responsible for payment of these expenses without regard to liability. In other words, workers' compensation is a no-fault coverage. Workers' compensation must be written as a separate policy. The coverage is mandatory in most states, and limits are statutory. The premium at the inception of the policy is based on payroll recorded by the insured and anticipated in the coming year, and the policy is subject to audit at its expiration, meaning that the insurance carrier will request actual payroll reports and other payroll information from the insured in order to determine the accuracy of the payroll reported. This is called a carrier audit. This may result in increased premium should the carrier find that the actual payroll is greater than the reported payroll.

Most workers' compensation policies include coverage for employer's liability, which should be purchased for situations in which lawsuits are brought against the library for employment-related suits not covered by the workers' compensation statutes. The standard policy will include an employer's liability limit of $100,000 per claim for employee injury that does not come within the Workers' Compensation Act.

In the states of North Dakota, Ohio, Washington, West Virginia, and Wyoming, and in Puerto Rico and the U.S. Virgin Islands, this insurance must be purchased from the state fund. In all other states, coverage is normally provided by private insurance companies. In those instances where the workers' compensation statute is not mandatory, the library should elect to come within the act if it can. This will guarantee benefits to employees injured on the job and will bar a common-law action for injuries.

Workers' Compensation Rates

The rates for workers' compensation are computed annually by occupational category based on actual experience in each individual state. Libraries usually will have employees in two classes, and most states use the following coding to identify them:

- Rating Code 8838—librarians or professional assistants, including clerical
- Rating Code 9101—all other employees (This is typically a catch-all classification that would include all nonprofessional employees. This may include custodians, janitors, and drivers.)

If the library has employees who do not fit into the categories defined above, the risk management consultant, agent, or broker can work with the library to determine the appropriate workers' compensation code.

In most cases, insurance companies have some flexibility in rating. The library's actual loss experience will be important. The premium paid at the inception of the policy is considered a deposit premium, and a final adjustment based on actual payroll is necessary at the expiration of the policy.

DIRECTORS' OR TRUSTEES' AND OFFICERS' LIABILITY

Directors' or trustees' and officers' liability is another area of liability risk to which directors, trustees, and officers may be subject and which is not covered by the standard general liability insurance policy. This is a risk like that intended to be covered by the directors' and officers' (D&O) policy written for business corporations. This type of policy undertakes to protect the directors and officers who might be sued by a shareholder on behalf of the corporation in a derivative action where the directors or officers have acted negligently or with poor business judgment and caused financial loss to the corporation. While the risks faced by a library's board may not be the same as a major for-profit corporation, people are generally reluctant to accept appointments to boards without D&O coverage.

There are three forms of coverage that may be applicable, depending on the nature of the library's legal status; that is, whether it is a nonprofit corporation, part of a governmental body, or part of a public school district. The coverage described is not included or generally available in the standard general liability insurance policy. Relatively few insurance companies provide this special coverage.

Directors' or Officers' and Trustees' Policy

This form is most appropriate for a private, nonprofit corporation or organization. The coverage applies to liability for a wrongful act, which is usually defined as

- any actual or alleged error or misstatement;
- misleading statement or act;
- omission or neglect;
- breach of duty by the directors, officers, or trustees in the discharge of their duties; or
- any matter claimed against them solely by reason of their being directors, officers, or trustees of the organization.

This is generally construed to include violations of civil and constitutional rights, although the policy will apply only to directors, officers, and trustees and will not defend employees who are not officers unless specifically endorsed. There are numerous exclusions, including the personal injury liability risks that can be separately insured under the general liability policy; liability resulting from failure to purchase insurance; liability for fraudulent or dishonest acts; and liability for acts resulting in personal gain. When the corporation or public institution has adopted a bylaw provision for indemnifying officers and directors for liability for these acts, the policy also will provide insurance for the corporation or public institution.

Public Officials' Liability

This policy provides similar coverage and is appropriate for municipally owned and other public libraries. The coverage applies to liability for wrongful act, which is defined essentially the same as in the directors' or officers' and trustees' policy. Usually, it can be extended to include employees as insureds. This may be especially important to administrators and others in a supervisory capacity because it may present the only opportunity to provide coverage for these persons for civil and constitutional rights violations.

Board of Education, Public School Trustee, or Professional Liability

This coverage may be available for libraries that are part of a public school system. Usually, it may be extended to insure library employees.

EMPLOYMENT PRACTICES LIABILITY

Claims can be brought against a library for alleged violations of rights granted by several civil rights acts passed during the latter half of the twentieth century. Such claims can result from wrongful termination, discrimination, or retaliation based on age, gender, sexual orientation, race, religion, or country of national origin. Such claims can be costly to defend, with legal expenses sometimes exceeding the cost of an award or a settlement. The policy typically includes defense cost coverage. Employment practices coverage can be purchased as a stand-alone policy or endorsed onto a D&O policy or a public officials liability policy.

Such policies usually contain a self-insured retention (SIR) clause that is to be paid by the insured in the event of loss. The policies may be on a claims-made basis; that is, the policy covers claims made or first discovered during the term of the policy. This is in contrast with other liability policies that provide coverage if the accident or act complained of occurred during the policy term, even though the claim is made after the policy has expired, that is, occurrence based as discussed above.

FIDUCIARY LIABILITY

These policies may be written on a claims-made basis. This means that the policy will only cover claims first made against the library during the policy period. The policies may include HIPAA (Health Insurance Portability and Accountability Act of 1996, as amended) liability, and coverage for any penalties as a result of HIPAA violations, or violations of ERISA (Employee Retirement Income Security Act of 1974, as amended). If the policy includes HIPAA liability coverage, it will include liability as a result of HIPAA violations. Exclusions typically include an intentionally dishonest or fraudulent act or omission, or a willful violation of any statute, rule, or law.

CYBER LIABILITY POLICIES

Cyber liability policies provide coverage for claims involving cyber breaches. These policies provide breach response services, legal, forensic, and public relations/crisis management. Cyber policies have evolved over the years and will include first party loss coverage, that is, coverage for the direct cost to the library of business interruption losses resulting from either a security breach or from a system failure (due to the introduction of malware). The coverage may also include cyber extortion coverages as well as data recovery costs. Under the cyber liability portion of the policy, the coverage will also include cyber/network privacy liability, regulatory defense and penalties, and payment card liabilities and costs. Some policies also provide coverage for "e-Crime." At the time of this writing, this is an ever-evolving market. A library's risk manager or an insurance professional can provide ongoing advice about coverage improvements and enhancements. Exclusions typically include asbestos, pollution, contamination, and war and civil war. Terrorism insurance coverage is available.

TERRORISM INSURANCE COVERAGE

In response to the catastrophic impacts of the terrorist attacks against multiple targets on September 11, 2001, Congress passed the Terrorism Risk Insurance Act of 2002 as amended (TRIA). (Check for the latest amended version of the act.) This federal legislation provides insurance coverage arising out of defined acts of terrorism. Many types of insurance coverages, including property, workers' compensation, and liability, may include TRIA coverage. TRIA requires all insurance companies that offer property and casualty insurance policies to offer property and casualty insurance coverage for losses resulting from terrorism on terms and conditions that do not differ materially from the general policy's terms and conditions. TRIA coverage is voluntary and will require additional premium. The insurance policies that provide TRIA options will provide TRIA endorsements including a description of the coverage and a reference to federal statutes. For TRIA to be triggered, the act must be certified by the federal government as an act of terrorism. The TRIA statute does have an expiration date, which is provided in the insurance policy's TRIA endorsement. Congress has extended the act's coverage over the years since 9/11 in a series of amendments.

VOLUNTEERS

Some liability insurance policies do provide coverage protection for volunteers who are named in lawsuits. The protection is similar to that provided to employees who are covered for their actions while in the course and scope of their employment. Similarly, volunteers may be afforded comparable protection for their actions while in the course and scope of their volunteer activities.

Workers' compensation will not cover volunteers who are injured while performing their volunteer activities, because workers' compensation insurance is designed for library employees. The medical payments coverage described earlier in the general liability section may be used to cover the medical expenses for volunteers who are injured on the library's premises. This type of coverage is a no-fault coverage, and as described earlier is subject to policy conditions and low limits. In the case of volunteers injured while performing service for the library, this allows the library to reimburse a volunteer for some or all of the medical bills resulting from the injury.

Volunteers who use their personal vehicles for their volunteer activities are typically not covered by the library's auto liability insurance. Volunteers' personal auto policies will be expected to respond to any auto accident.

It is possible to obtain specialty stand-alone insurance to cover volunteers. This type of coverage may include both volunteer liability coverage as well as volunteer accident coverage. This type of coverage is confined to activities that the volunteer performs on behalf of the library. Many volunteer accident insurance policies are excess over an individual's personal health insurance.

POLICY DOCUMENT RETENTION

All liability policies should be maintained in a permanent archive. Do not rely on insurance brokers or insurance carriers to maintain copies of historic, archived insurance policies. Discussion with IT staff about any policies stored electronically is critical.

7

New Construction

New construction projects create new and unusual risks for the library. They also afford an opportunity to apply the concepts of risk management to the library's advantage. Cooperation between the architect and the insurance agent, engineer, or consultant before the plans are finalized may help reduce fire hazards and make the premises safer. Delineating insurance requirements for the contractor will shift the risk of claims for accidents to the one whose activity is likely to cause those accidents.

The insurance considerations discussed in this chapter may apply to remodeling and maintenance contracts as well as to major construction projects.

INSURANCE REVIEW OF ARCHITECT'S PLANS

Architects should be aware of, and familiar with, building and safety code requirements. They should be required to work with the library's insurance agent, consultant, broker, or the insurance company's engineer, and have the insurance company review and approve the plans.

INSURANCE REQUIREMENTS FOR ARCHITECTS

The architect should generally carry the same coverage as listed below for the contractor. Additionally, an architect should be required to provide evidence of professional or errors and omissions, liability insurance, commonly called Architects E&O. Evidence of insurance is typically a certificate of insurance that is issued by the architect's insurance broker or agent. This policy covers claims arising out of the negligent acts, errors, and omissions by the consultant, subconsultant, or anyone directly or indirectly employed by them. The coverage provided should not be less than $1 million on projects up to $5 million, or 20 percent of the value for projects costing more than $5 million.

INSURANCE REQUIREMENTS FOR THE CONTRACTOR

Before commencing construction, the contractor should be required to furnish certificates of insurance for

- workers' compensation and employer's liability;
- general liability, including contractual liability (insuring the indemnity clause described below) and completed operations (which applies to accidents occurring after completion as a result of defects in the structure); and
- comprehensive auto liability.

Required policy limits should be at least equal to the limits purchased by the library on its own general and auto liability policies.

OWNERS' PROTECTIVE LIABILITY INSURANCE

A contingent liability coverage known as owners' protective liability is designed to protect the owner (the library) in the event there is a question as to whether an accident arose out of the construction project (and therefore is within the indemnity agreement). Sometimes owners and general contractors may be sued for the actions of subcontractors that have been hired and supervised by them. Some construction contracts will require the contractor to furnish an owners' protective policy in the name of the library. More often, the library will purchase this coverage as part of its general liability policy, in which case the coverage will be described as independent contractor's coverage. The premium is based on the amount of the contract.

HOLD HARMLESS

An indemnity (hold harmless) clause should be included in both the architect consulting and construction contracts. Because the owner (library) is usually liable for accidents on its premises when work is being performed, the indemnity clause is necessary to shift the responsibility for injuries back to the architect who designed the project or the contractor who has charge of the work. Here are two samples:

- Architects hold harmless: The consultant agrees to defend, indemnify, and hold harmless the owner, its officers, agents, and employees from and against all losses and expenses (including costs and attorney's fees) resulting from any injury (including death) to any person, or damages to property of others arising out of the negligent acts, errors, or omissions of the consultant, its employees, or agents in performance of the work under this agreement.
- Contractor hold harmless: The contractor agrees to defend, indemnify, and hold harmless the owner, its officers, agents, and employees from and against all losses and expenses (including costs and attorney's fees) resulting from any injury (including death) to any person, or damages to property of others arising out of the negligent acts of the contractor, its employees, subcontractors, or agents in performance of the work under this agreement.

SURETY (PERFORMANCE) BOND

Unlike an insurance policy, which is a two-party contract between insured and insurer, bonds are three-party written agreements—the general contractor is the principal, the owner (or library) is the obligee, and the bonding company is the surety. Public bodies generally are required by statute to secure a bond from the contractor guaranteeing performance of the contract, usually in the amount of the contract. This is protection against insolvency during the job, but also against the risk of liens that might be levied against the property for work or materials of subcontractors and suppliers whom the contractor has failed to pay. Private libraries and institutions also are well-advised to consider the protection of such a bond.

There are other types of bonds common in construction. While a performance bond guarantees performance under a contract, labor and material bonds guarantee the labor and materials owed by the general contractor (principal.) Like a performance bond, labor and material bonds are often required by public bodies.

BUILDER'S RISK INSURANCE

Builder's risk insurance covers a building during the course of construction. Because both the builder and the library have an insurable interest in the project during construction, it is most economical to insure both interests in a single policy. The policy may be purchased by the library or the contractor, depending on the contract terms. Its essential features are as follows:

- the amount of coverage is usually the completed value of the building (a rate adjustment is allowed to compensate for the gradual increase in the amount at risk)
- the builder's risk policies generally provide all risk coverage
- a deductible in an amount of $10,000 or higher may be required on the builder's risk policy (Usually, responsibility for the deductible will fall on the contractor, who has the obligation to protect the property. A specific agreement between the parties on this point is desirable as part of the construction contract. Generally, the contractor has more control over the construction site, and it is common to have the contractor either provide the builder's risk policy, or at a minimum, to be responsible for the deductible.)

The builder's risk policy is intended to apply only during construction. Care should be taken in the wording of the construction contracts on when builder's risk ends. Some builder's risk insurance policies will end on occupancy. There may be situations where new construction is under partial occupancy, but the construction is not completed. The builder and the library may still have an insurable interest in the ongoing construction, and so the builder's risk policy should not end. In situations such as these, it is common to request a "partial occupancy" endorsement to the builder's risk policy.

Once the building is completed and ready for occupancy, the insurance company that provides the library's blanket real and personal property coverage should be notified so that coverage for the new building can be added to that policy. Where construction involves remodeling of, or adding to, an existing building, a builder's risk policy may not be necessary because the blanket building and contents form automatically includes additions and alterations.

If the contract is for a substantial amount, it may be necessary to increase the amount of insurance under the blanket policy as the work progresses.

LEED OR "GREEN" CONSTRUCTION

New construction commonly includes environmentally responsible best practices. Leadership in Energy and Environmental Design (LEED) is one of the most commonly acceptable certification programs. Projects may qualify for a number of categories under LEED.

Most insurance policies—whether a property insurance policy or a builder's risk policy—will provide coverage to ensure that cost of construction includes the costs of compliance to current building codes. Insurance coverage to include any additional expenses related to LEED certification or "green" construction practices may not automatically be included. For new construction that is LEED-certified, the library should work with its insurance professionals to ensure that its property policies are adequately endorsed.

8
Claims

Indemnity, a basic principle of insurance, provides protection from liabilities incurred by one's actions, but importantly states that the insured should not profit from a covered loss. Insurance should restore the customer to approximately the same financial position that existed before any loss occurred.

The insurance adjuster will be a key person in connection with losses and claims, although the cooperation of the library staff is also essential. An important part of the insurance program is the assignment of responsibility for reporting losses and accidents that might result in claims. This includes instructions as to how and to whom these reports are to be made.

The claims process, in essence, brings the risk management process full circle. Good and thorough risk identification and quantification will make the loss adjustment process considerably easier for everyone.

The insurance carrier will only pay for covered losses or expenses up to the limits of the insurance purchased. This applies to all types of coverage. For example, if the library were to purchase crime insurance of $50,000, with a $5,000 deductible, and $100,000 was stolen, the maximum the insurance carrier is required to cover is $50,000 less any deductibles. The library would be responsible for the deductible, plus any additional amounts in addition of the limits; that is, the library would be responsible for $55,000.

PROMPT REPORTING OF LOSSES AND ACCIDENTS

Most policies require the insurer to be notified of losses and accidents quickly. This is necessary for proper claim handling. Liability insurance policies will specify the circumstances when the insurer must be notified. Failure to notify an insurance carrier in a timely fashion (as provided in the insurance policy) may lead to a denial of coverage.

The library should have an internal process whereby losses and accidents are reported internally. And the library should clearly identify the person(s) responsible to report claims to the insurer. There may be different people responsible for claim reporting, sometimes depending on the line of coverage. For example, there may be different people responsible for reporting workers' compensation claims and property claims.

MAJOR PROPERTY LOSSES

The timely and proper assessment of any claim depends on the availability of complete documentation. (See the list of these documents discussed later in this section.) If the library has all of the necessary documents, the library and the adjuster will have little problem agreeing on the value of the library's lost or damaged property.

The steps taken immediately after a loss will affect the library's ability to return to normal operations as quickly as possible and to determine the extent of the damage and the valuation of the property damaged or lost. Prompt action is critical to prevent damaged property from damaging undamaged property.

After notifying the claims adjuster of the loss, the following steps are necessary before the value of the loss can be determined:

- mobilize the emergency organization
- protect the library's property from further damage
- repair leaking pipes
- restore fire protection
- temporarily support collapsed or impaired structures
- board up the premises and correct unsafe conditions if they exist
- isolate the damaged area wherever possible
- separate damaged from undamaged property

- restore power to critical areas, such as freezers
- establish a loss account in the library's books, and charge all expenses incurred as a result of the loss to this account
- retain all invoices, time sheets, and so on to ensure that all costs are captured and attributed to the loss
- retain any pieces of equipment or property that may be the cause of the loss
- do not dispose of any damaged property until the claims adjuster has had an opportunity to inspect it
- take photos prior to the removal of any debris

In order to document the value of library property, the library should have the following paperwork:

- invoices
- purchase orders
- repair quotations
- time and materials contracts with expenditures
- labor time sheets with corresponding payroll journals
- supply vouchers or requisitions
- inventory quantities with pricing
- contracts for the property of others, confirming insurable interest

Finally, losses that include business interruption, loss of revenue, and extra expenses require the following additional information:

- additional expenses incurred to reduce the period of suspension of operations
- reconstruction schedule
- actual expenses and revenue, during the indemnity period
- actual expenses and revenue, immediately prior to the loss, usually for a one-year period
- budgetary projections for the time of loss and a period of time beyond the date of loss

Special Collections, Rare Books and Manuscripts, and Valuable Papers and Records

The library can minimize damage to rare materials by establishing a conservation service agreement before any loss occurs. Because most of the repairable property damage in a fire is caused by water, immediate attention to water damage can drastically reduce the cost of restoring materials to their pre-disaster condition. A visual record of the condition of the most valuable materials before the loss can help to determine the amount of conservation treatment covered by insurance claims.

For very old materials that may already have damage or considerable wear, it is difficult to determine the actual cost of conservation for a known incident without having first established the items' pre-disaster condition. If this precaution is not taken, disputes could result, impeding the chances for a prompt and amicable settlement. In the case of irreplaceable materials, the loss of a single item could be substantial. Establishing not only the value, but also the general condition on a yearly basis is key to settlement.

In any major loss adjustment, it is a great advantage to the library to be able to demonstrate to the loss adjuster that careful thought and study were given to the subject of values before the insurance was written. The total valuation summary should include a value for every significant category of materials. In the event that materials damaged or destroyed cannot be replaced with other copies, then loss adjustment will be in the amount which allows the library to acquire materials of similar kind and utility.

In every case where the library assumes or incurs responsibility for the property of others, the library should endeavor to get replacement-cost values from the owners. Although courts may hesitate to enforce a clause or waiver eliminating the responsibility of the library, they generally will sustain an agreement as to the value in the event of a loss. When an item is irreplaceable and there is no ready market for similar items, the value may be purely arbitrary and may depend on whether the proposed value is reasonable and how much premium the library is willing to pay for insurance. By insuring such items on a valued policy or agreed amount form, the insurance company accepts the stated value as the amount of loss if the item is stolen or destroyed.

Salvage

Damage to books resulting from a fire loss usually involves extensive water damage. Sophisticated salvage procedures have been developed that involve freeze-drying to prevent mold, and vacuum-drying. However, whether salvage is practical will depend upon several circumstances to be discussed between the library and loss adjuster.

For those books that are very valuable and irreplaceable, the library may be willing to accept the salvaged product, even though scars of the damage remain. For books that are replaceable, the decision to replace them (or salvage them) will depend on the replacement costs as these relate to salvage expense and condition after salvage. Salvage expense should include handling costs, reprocessing, and filing, as well as the contract costs for the salvage process.

Proof of Loss

Most property policies require proof of loss to be filed within a certain time period, although the insurer may extend this time limit if requested to do so by the insured. However, in any loss where there is a serious question of coverage, the library should comply with the provision or secure a written extension from the insurance company's loss adjuster.

Insurance Carrier Inspections or Site Visits after a Loss

An insurance carrier may at its option have its claims adjuster inspect the damage and visit the site after the loss. This is usually where the claim is extensive or large. The library and its staff as the insureds have an obligation to cooperate with the insurance carrier and its representative. Be prepared to answer questions and provide information in order to support the library's claims. It is preferable to ensure that the library's risk manager or broker accompany the claims adjuster to the site and attend any meetings between the claims adjuster and the library and facility staff.

CRIME

The library should report losses as a result of crime to the insurance company as soon as it is aware that these have occurred. Sometimes losses as a result of criminal activity such as embezzlement or fraud may take several years before they come to light. The information typically required by the insurance carrier includes

- date of discovery of the loss;
- description of the loss;
- individuals (if known) responsible for the loss;
- all records to support and verify the amount of loss;
- copies of police reports, and status updates of law enforcement investigation; and
- status of any recovery.

The insurance carrier may at its option seek reimbursement for any monies paid under the insurance policy to the library from the wrongdoer if identified and if found. If the library is successful at recovering monies, it is required to reimburse any portion that was paid by the insurance carrier.

After a reasonable amount of time once loss has been discovered and reported, the insurance carrier will expect the library to report

- the outcome of any criminal trial, sentencing including restitution and
- the measures implemented to prevent this type of loss from reoccurring.

WORKERS' COMPENSATION

Coverage requires an "employer's first report of injury" to satisfy the Industrial Commission or other state body that is responsible for administering workers' compensation benefits. Each state has different reporting requirements. Failure to report may result in state statutory penalties.

Generally, the "First Report of Injury" will include the following information:

- date of injury
- date of report of injury
- name of injured employee
- name of supervisor
- description of event causing injury
- names of any witnesses
- description of injury and whether medical treatment was sought

In order to be eligible under workers' compensation, the injury must arise from the employee's work. Personal health conditions are not covered by workers' compensation.

The claims adjuster assigned to the claim will investigate the claim to ensure whether it is compensable under the state statute and case law. In addition, the claims adjuster will ensure that all parties involved comply with all statutory requirements during the course of the claim. The insurance company will pay the injured employee's covered medical bills, lost wages, and, if appropriate, any additional benefit. The goal is to get the injured worker back to work in the safest manner possible. An injured worker may be returned to work with restrictions. It is important that both the injured worker and their supervisor understand the restrictions and ensure that the employee works within those restrictions to avoid re-injury.

CYBER

The library should notify the insurance carrier as soon as it has any actual or reasonably suspected data breach or security breach, as soon as reasonably possible after a cyber extortion threat is received, or after the discovery of an e-Crime. The insurance policy will specify conditions for notice to the insurance carrier.

Cyber insurance policies often contain other services that are useful in supporting the library during these types of incidents. Other services could include credit monitoring for impacted individuals, cyber forensic expertise, and other post-breach remedial services.

The insurance carrier will only pay the insured for covered losses and expenses, up to the limit of insurance purchased less any deductible.

AUTO ACCIDENTS

Most states require that auto accidents be reported on a standard accident form. The normal time limit is twenty-four hours from the time of the accident if bodily injury is involved, and ten days if only property damage occurs. The state form is usually acceptable to the insurance company.

Keep accident reporting instructions in the glove compartment of the vehicle, along with the vehicle's proof of insurance. It is very important for library employees not to make any statements at the scene of the accident that could be construed as admitting fault.

The following information should be collected at the scene of accident (if it involves another party or parties):

- the driver's license information of all drivers involved
- the auto insurance information of all vehicles involved
- make note and take pictures of damage to the vehicles involved in the accident
- make note and take pictures of any debris from the accident, and where it is placed
- make note and take pictures of the placement of vehicles upon impact
- ensure that you obtain the details and contact information of any witnesses
- if possible, make note of any injuries, or any individuals reporting injuries

Since smartphones are ubiquitous, using a smartphone to take photos of any damage to vehicles involved and taking photos of the scene where the accident occurred is recommended, if possible.

Often after an auto accident, a person may feel quite shocked and shaken up. As soon as practically possible the library employees should write down in their own words what happened, and any other details about the accident that they remember. It is important to do this as soon as possible after the accident, as over time important facts may be forgotten. This will be useful should they be contacted by the library's insurance carrier, or by the other party's insurance carrier, or if they are required to appear in court.

Library employees should not speak with the auto insurance claims adjusters of other parties, unless they have first received approval from the library's risk management professionals or legal counsel. If approached, it is best to simply refer the adjusters to the library's legal counsel.

A library employee may be cited for a traffic violation at the scene of the accident. The library should require as an internal policy that all motor vehicle accidents, including ones that result in traffic violations, are reported internally, in addition to reporting the accident per state requirements. It is important that the employee comply with all requests to appear in court. Depending on whether the employee disputes the citation, they may wish to obtain their own legal representation.

Auto insurance will not cover criminal violations, including the penalties and fines associated with traffic violations.

OTHER LIABILITY

All injuries to persons on library premises should be reported internally. The incident reports, however, should be made by the librarian and kept on file in the event a claim is later filed. It is desirable to discuss the reporting of such incidents with the insurance company, agent, or broker in order to develop guidelines to be followed. In the case of slips, trips, or falls, whether it is a claim or a non-reportable incident, the librarian should investigate the incident. The report should indicate the nature of the incident, the alleged cause, and whether the librarian corroborates the cause. For example, if a patron states that a fall was caused by water on a stairway, the librarian should immediately inspect the stairway to confirm the report. In some instances, it may be wise to take a photograph of the area to keep on file.

It is important for library employees not to make any statements to patrons who may have suffered damage or sustained injury that could later be construed as admitting fault or admitting that the library is negligent.

LAWSUITS AGAINST THE LIBRARY

Some types of liability claims commence with a plaintiff filing a lawsuit against the library. For public entities, there may be notice requirements and other procedures that need to be followed by plaintiffs. If a library employee is served with legal proceedings or an attorney letter of demand is received, it is important to refer those proceeding to the library's attorneys, or risk manager, or insurance carrier as appropriate.

Attorney-Client Privilege

It is common in situations where there is a claim or a lawsuit against the library for the library to seek legal advice. Legal advice may include

- actions that need to be taken in preparation for the library's defense, including investigation of the claims or lawsuit brought against the library;
- the preservation of records, e-mails, and other documents that will be used in an upcoming trial;
- opinions concerning the library's legal liability; and
- communications around possible options or outcomes that may or may not involve a settlement.

All communication between the library and its legal counsel for the purpose of securing legal advice is "privileged" communication. This means that all communication is confidential. Attorney-client privilege allows for the library to receive candid advice and effective legal representation. The library should have established protocols regarding communications around obtaining legal advice on how to handle and investigate liability claims and lawsuits.

There is extensive case law around this doctrine and its exceptions. The library should consult further with its legal counsel if it has any questions about which communications are privileged and how best to proceed.

Cooperation with the Liability Insurance Company

As the insured, the library has a duty to cooperate with its insurance company in claims investigation and handling. The library must do everything reasonable to mitigate its own damages. It must not do anything to prejudice the insurance carrier's rights under the insurance policy.

In general, the liability insurance company steps into the shoes of the library when a claim for injury is presented. This is true unless the library has a significant self-insured retention (SIR). An SIR is like a deductible in that the insured (the library) is responsible for the amount of the SIR. Generally, however, in the event of a deductible, the insurance company handles the claim and pays the net of the deductible. With an SIR, the insured library is responsible for claim handling, with an obligation to report claims of certain types or above a certain amount; this is typically any claim that may result in a resolution greater than the amount of the SIR and, therefore, would involve a payment by the insurance company in addition to the SIR.

When the claim has been submitted to the insurance company, the insurer has the legal right to full cooperation of the library's personnel in the defense of a claim or suit against the library. If there is a clear-cut case of liability, the insurance company will generally be anxious to settle with the claimant. However, settlement is the prerogative of the company, and the library should not make any commitments.

Because a claim may exceed the SIR, and the insurance company may ultimately handle all aspects of liability and workers' compensation claims, it is important that all papers and communications that come to the library should be passed on promptly to the insurance company. These may include bills, medical reports, claim letters, summons, and complaints constituting lawsuits.

Defense Costs

One of the most important reasons for a library to purchase liability insurance (and the different types of liability insurance more fully described in chapter 6) is that liability insurance covers defense costs. The insurance policy will describe whether the insurance carrier has a duty to defend, or whether it has a duty to pay. The library need only show that there is potential for coverage under the policy in order to trigger the insurer's duty to defend. It does not matter if the lawsuit results in no damages awarded; the insurance carrier will still have a duty to defend. Insurance policies will spell out explicitly how much control the insurance carrier will assume in the defense process, including the selection of counsel. Duty to pay policies require that the insurance carrier reimburse the library for defense costs incurred defending the claim.

Bibliography

Adams, John F. 1972. *Risk Management and Insurance Guidelines for Higher Education*. Washington, DC: National Association of College and University Business Officers.

Adams Becker, S., M. Cummins, A. Davis, A. Freeman, C. Hall Giesinger, V. Ananthanarayanan, K. Langley, and N. Wolfson. 2017. *NMC Horizon Report: 2017 Library Edition*. Austin, TX: New Media Consortium.

Bailey, Dan A. 2006. *Fiduciary Liability Loss Prevention*. Warren, NJ: Chubb Group of Insurance Companies. https://fliphtml5.com/lnht/orxg/basic.

Bernstein, Peter L. 1996. *Against the Gods: The Remarkable Story of Risk*. Hoboken, NJ: John Wiley & Sons.

Breighner, Mary. 1997. "Colleges and University Can Take on Mother Nature . . . and Win." *URMIA Journal* 1:1–5.

Breighner, Mary, Barbara Carlson, and Gerald Naylis. 1998. "Modern Loss Control Protects Campus Value." *URMIA Journal* 2: 31–37.

Breighner, Mary, Jeanne Drewes, and Gerry Alonso. 2001. "Understanding Property Insurance Values." *URMIA Journal* 5: 43–51.

Breighner, Mary, William Payton, and Jeanne Drewes. 2005. *Risk and Insurance Management Manual for Libraries*. Chicago: American Library Association.

Campus Crime Prevention Programs. 2001. *Complete Library Safety and Security Manual: A Comprehensive Resource Manual for Academic and Public Library Professionals and Law Enforcement*. Goshen, KY: Campus Crime Prevention Programs.

Committee on Sponsoring Organizations of the Treadway Commission (COSO). 2004. "Enterprise Risk Management-Integrated Framework, Executive Summary." September. https://www.coso.org/Documents/COSO-ERM -Executive-Summary.pdf.

Eldred, Heather. 2007. "Do Friends Groups Need to Be Insured?" *Library Administrators Digest* 42, no. 2 (February): 11.

Federal Bureau of Investigation (FBI). n.d. "Active Shooter Resources." FBI. https://www.fbi.gov/about/partnerships/office-of-partner-engagement/ active-shooter-resources.

Frisz, Michael, and Mary Breighner. 1996. "Maintain Effective Loss Control on Campus During Downsizing." *URMIA Journal* 1: 4–11.

Goshay, Robert C. 1964. *Corporate Self-insurance and Risk Retention Plans, with General Reference to Fire, Liability, and Women's Compensation Exposures*. Homewood, Il.: S.S. Huebner Foundation for Insurance Education, PA: University of Pennsylvania.

Great American Insurance Group. "Loss Prevention Safety Topics: Cyber Security Tips" (brochure). https://www.greatamericaninsurancegroup.com/docs/default -source/loss-prevention/f13883-cyber-security-checklist-08-14-13-web .pdf?sfvrsn=f76977b1_4

Han, Zhengbiao, Shuiqing Huang, Huan Li, and Ni Ren. 2016. "Risk Assessment of Digital Library Information Security: A Case Study." *The Electronic Library* 34, no. 3. Emerald.com. https://www.emerald.com/insight/content/doi/10.1108/ EL-09-2014-0158/full/html.

Hubbard, Douglas W. 2009. *The Failure of Risk Management: Why It's Broken and How to Fix It*. Hoboken, NY: John Wiley & Sons.

Insurance Information Institute. 1989. *Sharing the Risk: How the Nation's Businesses, Homes, and Autos Are Insured*. 3rd rev. ed. New York: Insurance Information Institute.

———. 2010. *Insurance Handbook: A Guide to Insurance, What It Does, and How It Works*. New York: Insurance Information Institute.

Insurance Institute of America. 1980. *Readings in Risk Management*. Malvern, PA: The Institute.

International Organization for Standardization (ISO). 2018. *Risk Management—Guidelines*. ISO 31000. https://www.iso.org/obp/ ui/#iso:std:iso:31000:ed-2:v1:en.

Kenton, Will. 2019. "Enterprise Risk Management (ERM)." Investopedia, July 2. https://www.investopedia.com/terms/e/enterprise-risk-management.asp.

Kenton, Will. 2020. "Risk Assessment." Investopedia, May 27. https://www .investopedia.com/terms/r/risk-assessment.asp.

Layne, Olivia. "A Nonprofit's Guide to Risk Management." nonprofit hub, July 17, 2019. https://nonprofithub.org/ resources/a-nonprofits-guide-to-risk-management/.

Levine, Capron, and Bryan M. Carson. 2012. "Legally Speaking—Loss Prevention and Insurance." *Against the Grain* 24, no. 4 (September): 63–65.

Lewis, John B. 2009. *Employment Practices Loss Prevention Guidelines for Not-for-Profit Organizations: A Practical Guide from Chubb Executive Risk*. Warren, NJ: Chubb Group of Insurance Companies.

Library Administrator's Digest. 2011. "Police Investigate Stolen E.C. Library Data." *Library Administrator's Digest* 46, no. 4 (April): 26–27.

———. 2015. "Friends of the Library Volunteers Asked to Pay for Book Sale Insurance." *Library Administrator's Digest* 50, no. 4 (April): 2.

———. 2015. "Cohocton Public Library Ontario Insurance Rejected Us." *Library Administrator's Digest* 50, no. 7 (September): 1.

Library and Book Trade Almanac. 2019. 64th ed. Medford, NJ: Information Today. (See its section on "Risk Management, Insurance, Book Prices.")

Library of Congress, Preservation Directorate. www.loc.gov/preservation/emergprep.

Matthiesen, Bradley W., Gary L. Wickert, and Douglas W. Lehrer. 2013. *Fundamentals of Insurance Coverage in All 50 States*. 4th ed. Huntington, NY: Juris.

Mehr, Robert Irwin. 1986. *Fundamentals of Insurance*. 2nd ed. Irwin Series in Financial Planning and Insurance. Homewood, IL: Irwin.

Michigan Municipal League. "Manual of Risk." www.mml.org/insurance/ risk_resources/docs/public_works_rg.doc.

Myers, Marcia J. 1991. *Insuring Library Collections and Buildings*. SPEC Kit 178. Washington, DC: Association of Research Libraries, Office of Management Services.

National Fire Protection Association (NFPA). 2001. *NFPA 909: Code for the Protection of Cultural Resources Properties—Museums, Libraries, and Places of Worship*. Quincy, MA: National Fire Protection Association.

Occupational Health and Safety Assessment Series (OHSAS). 1999. *Occupational Health and Safety Management Systems—Specification*. OHSAS 18001. https:// qsem.files.wordpress.com/2010/10/ohsas-18001.pdf.

Payne, Lizanne. 2007. *Library Storage Facilities and the Future of Print Collections in North America*. Report commissioned by OCLC Programs and Research. Dublin, OH. https://library.oclc.org/digital/collection/p267701coll27/id/327/.

Payton, Annie Malesia, and Theodosia T. Shields. 2008. "Insurance and Library Facilities." Special issue: "New Library Security for Buildings, Users, and Staff." *Library & Archival Security* 21, no. 2: 187–93.

Reed, B. J., and John W. Swain. 1990. *Public Finance Administration*. Englewood Cliffs, NJ: Prentice Hall.

Reeder, T. Jefferson, Editor, 1990. *Financial Accounting and Reporting Manual for Higher Education*. Washington, DC: National Association of College and University Business Officers.

Rejda, George E. 1992. *Principles of Risk Management and Insurance,* 4th ed. New York: HarperCollins.

Rejda, George E., Michael McNamara, and William Huitt Rabel. 2020. *Principles of Risk Management and Insurance*. Boston: Pearson Education.

Rouse, Margaret. 2017. "Risk Assessment." TechTarget. https://searchcompliance.techtarget.com/definition/risk-assessment.

Shaw, Seyfarth. 2005. *Employment Practices Loss Prevention Guidelines: A Practical Guide from Chubb*. Warren, NJ: Chubb Group of Insurance Companies.

Simmons, Heidi. 2018. "A Framework for the Analysis and Management of Library Security Issues Applied to Patron Property Theft." *Journal of Academic Librarianship* 44, no. 2 (March): 279–86.

Stamatis, D. H. 2019. *Advanced Product Quality Planning: The Road to Success*. Boca Raton, FL: CRC Press.

Strauch, Bruce, Bryan M. Carson, and Jack Montgomery. 2012. "Legally Speaking-Loss Prevention and Insurance: Best Practices in the Protection of Historical Archives," *Against the Grain* 24, no. 4: Article 29. https://doi.org/10.7771/2380-176X.6197.

Trupin, Jerome, and Arthur L. Flitner. 1998. *Commercial Property Insurance and Risk Management*. 5th ed. Malvern, PA: American Institute for Chartered Property and Casualty Underwriters.

U.S. Department of Labor, Employee Benefits Security Administration. 2005. "Compliance Assistance: ERISA of 1974." www.dol.gov/ebsa/compliance_assistance.html.

U.S. Department of Labor, Occupational Safety and Health Administration. "OSHA Home Page." www.osha.gov.

———. 1986. *Recordkeeping and Reporting Guidelines for Federal Agencies: Under the Williams-Steiger Occupational Safety and Health Act of 1970*. Washington, DC: Government Printing Office.

U.S. General Accounting Office. 2004. "Terrorism Insurance, Implementation of the Terrorism Risk Insurance Act of 2002." Report to the Chairman, Committee on Financial Services, U.S. House of Representatives. April. www.gao.gov/new .items/d04307.pdf.

Vaughan, Emmett J. 1982. *Fundamentals of Risk and Insurance.* 3rd ed. New York: Wiley.

Velasquez, Diane L., Nina Evans, and Joanne Kaeding. 2016. "Risk Management and Disaster Recovery in Public Libraries in South Australia: A Pilot Study." *Information Research* 21, no. 4, paper 735. http://InformationR.net/ir/21-4/paper735 .html.

Wikipedia, "ISO 31000," Wikipedia, The Free Encyclopedia, last edited May 16, 2020, https://en.wikipedia.org/wiki/ISO_31000#:~:text=Definitions.

Williams, C. Arthur, and Richard M. Heins. 1985. *Risk Management and Insurance.* 5th ed. New York: McGraw-Hill.

APPENDIX A
Risk Management and Insurance Resources

This list is for general information and does not constitute an endorsement by the authors and editors.

GENERAL INFORMATION

Insurance Information Institute (III)
110 William St.
New York, NY 10038
Tel. (212) 346-5500
www.iii.org

Nonprofit Risk Management Center
"Glossary of Risk Management & Insurance Terms"
https://nonprofitrisk.org/resources/miscellaneous/glossary-risk-management
-insurance-terms/Public Risk Management Association (PRIMA)
700 S. Washington St., Suite 218
Arlington, VA 22314
Tel. (703) 528-7701
www.primacentral.org

The Risk Management Society (RIMS)
1407 Broadway, 29th Floor
New York, NY 10018
Tel. (212) 286-9292
www.rims.org

University Risk Management and
Insurance Association (URMIA)
P.O. Box 1027
Bloomington, IN 47402
Tel. (812) 727-7130
Fax (812) 727-7129
www.urmia.org

RESOURCES ON RISK MANAGEMENT AND INSURANCE ISSUES FOR LIBRARIES

American Library Association
225 N. Michigan Ave., Suite 1300
Chicago, IL 60601
Tel. 1-800-545-2433
www.ala.org

American Society of Appraisers
Tel. 1-800-ASA VALU (1-800-272-8258)
www.appraisers.org

Antiquarian Booksellers' Association of America (ABAA)
20 W. 44th St., #507
New York, NY 10036
Tel. (212) 944-8291
www.abaa.org

Appraisal Institute
www.appraisalinstitute.org
The Appraisal Institute is the nation's largest professional association of real estate appraisers.

Blackwell's Book Services
www.blackwell.com
blackwells.co.uk/rarebooks/

CBIZ Valuation Services
www.cbiz.com/accounting-tax/services/advisory/valuation-advisory/real-estate-valuation

Duff and Phelps
www.duffandphelps.com/services/valuation
This firm offers valuation and consulting for financial reporting, federal, state, and local tax, and investment and risk management purposes.

The Library and Book Trade Almanac
(formerly *The Bowker Annual*)
http://books.infotoday.com/directories/Library-and-Book-Trade-Almanac.shtml

Marshall and Swift (previously Marshall and Swift/Boeckh)
Tel. (800) 426-1466
https://www.corelogic.com/solutions/marshall-swift.aspx

American Title Valuation at LOC website
www.loc.gov/preservation/emergprep/insurancevaluation.html

Foreign Title Valuation on ALA Site
https://alair.ala.org/bitstream/handle/11213/8099/LMPI%20Article%202017
.pdf?sequence=1&isAllowed=y

LOSS PREVENTION RESOURCES

Federal Emergency Management Agency (FEMA)
Federal Centre Plaza
500 C St. S.W.
Washington, DC 20472
Tel. (800) 525-0321
www.fema.gov/about

FM Global
270 Central Ave
Johnston, R.I. 02919-4949
www.fmglobal.com
FM Global is one of the world's largest commercial and industrial property insurance and risk management organizations specializing in property protection. The
company provides information regarding property loss prevention resources.

National Fire Protection Association (NFPA)
1 Batterymarch Park
Quincy, MA 02169-7471
Tel. (617) 770-3000
www.nfpa.org
The mission of the international nonprofit NFPA is to reduce the worldwide
burden of fire and other hazards on the quality of life by providing and advocat-
ing scientifically based consensus codes and standards, research, training, and
education.
      NFPA publishes more than 300 consensus codes and standards that are
intended to minimize the possibility and effects of fire and other risks. The
NFPA codes and standards, which are administered by more than 250 technical
committees comprising approximately 8,000 volunteers, are adopted and used
throughout the world. Some of the most useful codes are listed below.

www.nfpa.org/codes-and-standards/all-codes-and-standards/list-of-codes-and-standards

NFPA 1 Fire Code

NFPA 11A Standard for Medium- and High-Expansion Foam Systems

NFPA 12 Standard on Carbon Dioxide Extinguishing Systems

NFPA 12A Standard on Halon 1301 Fire Extinguishing Systems

   Author's Note: Regulations for gaseous protection systems have changed since 1997. Halon is no longer readily available, and carbon dioxide poses a life-safety issue.

NFPA 13 Standard for the Installation of Sprinkler Systems

NFPA 17 Standard for Dry Chemical Extinguishing Systems

NFPA 101 Life Safety Code

NFPA 232 Standard for the Protection of Records

NFPA 909 Code for the Protection of Cultural Resource Properties—Museums, Libraries, and Places of Worship

NFPA 914 Code for the Protection of Historic Structures

NFPA 1600 Standard on Continuity, Emergency, and Crisis Management

NFPA 1620 Standard for Pre-Incident Planning

APPENDIX B
Sample Risk Management and Insurance Policy

It is in the best interest of the [*insert name*] library to make every reasonable effort to protect the health and safety of employees of the library and the public from any hazards incidental to the operation of the library and to protect its resources and assets, including the library's building(s) and its collections, against losses arising out of injuries, accidents, destruction, and damages. Preservation of the library's assets and resources is a major responsibility of all employees. Managers are the custodians of the property that the library has entrusted to them, and they also are responsible for the safety of any persons who may directly or indirectly be affected by the library's operations. All persons with responsibility must, therefore, learn to manage those risks that could destroy or deplete their assets or that could harm any person. However, before these risks can be controlled, they must be recognized. To that end, the board shall establish risk management procedures to: identify risks; quantify and evaluate those risks; avoid them when possible without compromising the library's mission; take steps to reduce risks through loss prevention and control; and finance remaining risks by transferring them, when feasible, through appropriate agreements, the use budgeted of self-insurance, or the purchase of commercial insurance.

By appropriate resolution, the Board of Trustees of the [*insert name*] library on [*insert date*] has established the following policy in relation to its risk management and insurance program.

a. Responsibility for administering the risk management and insurance program shall rest with the administrator.

b. In accordance with the opening statement of this policy, it is the intention of this board to follow sound risk management practices. In that regard, the administrator is charged with the responsibility of identifying and quantifying the risks of loss to which the library is exposed; for developing, implementing, and overseeing a formal loss prevention program; and for developing and implementing a comprehensive risk financing program incorporating self-insurance and commercial insurance, including lines of coverage, and in amounts reasonable to protect the library's assets and resources. For strategic planning purposes, the administrator should report to the board on the risk management and insurance program on a periodic basis, but not less than once each year. The report shall include recommendations, if any, for preserving and protecting the library's property, a list of insured and uninsured losses that have occurred during the past year, and an indication of possible risks of loss for which insurance is not currently available or has not been purchased, as well as information regarding the current insurance program, including a description of lines of coverage, limits of liability, deductibles, and premium.

c.1. It is the policy of the board to insure catastrophic risks and to assume minor risks by budgeted self-insurance or by the use of deductibles, where appropriate. It is the desire of the board to limit aggregate annual self-insured losses to an acceptable percentage of the annual budget. Toward that end, the board, treasurer, or other individual designated by the board will make a budget allocation each year to cover anticipated self-insured losses.

c.2. The administrator may designate an insurance consultant, agent, or broker to assist in the risk management process and to act as risk management consultant as deemed necessary by the administrator. The consultant, agent, or broker shall secure quotes from financially responsible insurance companies periodically as directed by the administrator. The consultant, agent, or broker's compensation will be negotiated by the administrator directly with the consultant, agent, or broker. (Note: this responsibility may be subject to approval of the board or it may be delegated to the administrator or other person without needing the approval of the board.)

d. The administrator shall promptly report all serious losses (as defined by the board) to the board.

APPENDIX C
Risk Assessment Template

RISK SCORING

Risk scoring can be as simple or as complex as you would like. Typically, risk scoring matrixes settle for simple, easy to understand parameters. Color coding is common, with scores in the yellow or red bands considered "actionable." (For example, in the following image the darker shades of gray are considered actionable.)

Name of Program: (*Describe the program.*)

Objective of Program: (*Describe the objectives of the program. Consider how the program aligns with the library's mission and values.*)

Date of Assessment:

Date of review (This should be a *future date.*):

Risk/Hazard	Likelihood	Impact	Risk Score	Strategies	Residual Risk	Resources Required	Who
Identify risks or hazards that may occur.	Consider the likelihood/probability of event occurring.	Consider human, facility, and mission impacts.	Likelihood × Impact	Describe strategies to minimize and reduce risk/hazard.	Describe any risks remaining after strategies have been implemented.	Identifies resources needed to successfully implement strategy to reduce risk.	Individuals or team responsible

5 x 5

Risk
Risk
1–5
6–10
11–15

	Likelihood				
Impact	**Negligible** (1)	**Rare** (2)	**Occasional** (3)	**Frequent** (4)	**Always** (5)
Negligible (1)	1	2	3	4	5
Low (2)	2	4	6	8	10
Medium (3)	3	6	9	12	15
High (4)	4	8	12	16	20
Extreme (5)	5	10	15	20	25

APPENDIX D
Suggested Guidelines in Library and Museum Security

AMERICAN SOCIETY FOR INDUSTRIAL SECURITY (ASIS) INTERNATIONAL

"Intelligent Surveillance Insights Protect Museum's Art Collection"
*www.asisonline.org/security-management-magazine/articles/2019/10/intelligent
-surveillance-insights-protect-museums-art-collection/*

ASSOCIATION OF COLLEGE AND RESEARCH LIBRARIES (ACRL)

"ACRL/RBMS Guidelines Regarding Security and Theft in Special Collections"
www.ala.org/acrl/standards/security_theft
These guidelines include information on marking and on interlibrary and exhibition loans of special collection materials.

MUSEUM ASSOCIATION SECURITY COMMITTEE

www.securitycommittee.org
The Museum Association Security Committee is the security committee for the American Alliance of Museums (AAM). Its mission is to serve the members and non-members of AAM by providing security expertise to the museum community. Many sections of its website that provide advice for museums are equally applicable to libraries:

- Welcome page: http://www.securitycommittee.org/securitycommittee/Welcome.html
- Guidelines and Standards: http://www.securitycommittee.org/securitycommittee/Guidelines_and_Standards.html
- Important Resources: http://www.securitycommittee.org/securitycommittee/Resources.html
- Protecting Historic Sites: http://www.securitycommittee.org/securitycommittee/Historic_Sites.html
- College Galleries: http://www.securitycommittee.org/securitycommittee/College_Galleries.html

APPENDIX E
Property Loss Prevention Checklist

Make certain these points (below) are part of the regular facility inspection; for example, annual inspections, or after any major event such as a hurricane, flood, or fire.

PERIMETER SECURITY

Is the perimeter kept free of unnecessary materials?
Yes _____ No _____
Is perimeter lighting working?
Yes _____ No _____
Are perimeter windows secured at all times?
Yes _____ No _____
Are perimeter doors secured upon closing?
Yes _____ No _____

HOUSEKEEPING

Are housekeeping staff included in training for prevention?
Yes _____ No _____
Are housekeeping staff included in documenting areas of risk?
Yes _____ No _____

FENCES

Is the fence in good repair?
Yes _____ No _____
If no, location of damage _____
Date corrected _____
Are combustible materials stacked away from the building?
Yes _____ No _____
If no, location of materials _____
Date corrected _____

ROOF

Is the roof in good repair?
Yes _____ No _____
If no, location of damage _____
Date corrected _____

WALLS/ROOF

Are walls and roof secured from vermin, birds, and bats?
Yes _____ No _____

FIRE ENGINE ACCESS

Are fire engine access lanes clear at all times?
Yes _____ No _____

LANDSCAPING

Are the grounds properly maintained, with fire-retardant plantings?
Yes _____ No _____

DUMPSTERS

Are dumpsters secured and stored away from buildings?
Yes _____ No _____
If no, location _____
Date corrected

GATES AND LOCKS

Are normally secured areas locked?
Yes _____ No _____
If no, location of gate _____
Date corrected _____

SECURITY LIGHTS

Interior Lights
Are interior lights working?
Yes _____ No _____
If no, location of faulty light _____
Date corrected

Exterior Lights
Are all exterior lights working?
Yes _____ No _____
If no, location of faulty light _____
Date corrected _____

TRASH COLLECTION

Is all the debris removed by the end of day?
Yes _____ No _____
If no, location of debris_____
Date corrected _____

DOORS/WINDOWS/LATCHES

Are all openings secured?
Yes _____ No _____
If no, location _____
Date corrected _____

AUTOMATIC FIRE PROTECTION

Are sprinklers clear of obstructions (for example, by high storage)?
Yes _____ No _____
If no, location of problem _____
Date corrected _____
Are sprinkler control valves locked in the open position?
Yes _____ No _____
If no, location of unlocked valve _____
Date/time corrected _____

OTHER POINTS

Immediately report to a supervisor any

- signs of tampering with doors, windows, or security and protective devices;
- occurrence of false burglar or fire alarms; and
- unescorted visitors in nonpublic areas.

APPENDIX F
Library Safety Inspection Checklist

This inspection checklist is designed to aid the [*name of library*] in providing a safe environment for the employees and patrons of the library. Where deficiencies are noted, please mark the individual line item with an "X" and explain your observations in the space provided under the individual sections.

This inspection should be done regularly, for example, annually or after any significant event.

Date of Inspection: _____

AREAS INSPECTED

____ Auditorium/facilities
____ Main floor
____ Second floor
____ Other floors as appropriate
____ Outside areas

Persons conducting the inspection: _____

EMERGENCY/FIRE PROTECTION

____ First-aid kits are readily accessible and stocked with adequate supplies.
____ AEDs (automatic external defibrillators) are regularly inspected.
____ Injury report packets are available with instructions/procedures wherever first-aid kits are located.
____ There is clear and unobstructed access to fire extinguishers.
____ Flammable/combustible materials are stored away from ignition sources.
____ Exits are clearly marked and recognizable from interior of building.
____ Exit aisleways and doorways are kept unobstructed.
____ Employees are trained in the use of fire extinguishers.

Explain any deficiencies noted above:

_____

BUILDING, STRUCTURES, AND OVERALL HOUSEKEEPING

____ Floors are in good condition without tripping hazards.
____ Stairways and handrails are in good condition.

____ Ramps/loading areas are in good condition and free from tripping hazards.
____ Guardrails are installed and in good condition at elevated platforms.
____ Materials are stored in a manner to prevent falling or collapsing.
____ Restrooms are clean; the shower and shower curtain are clean.
____ Waste disposal is timely in trash cans, restrooms, offices, outside areas, and so on.
____ Sidewalks and parking lot are free of large cracks and tripping hazards.
____ Landscaping is regularly maintained to avoid any hazards.
____ Chairs, tables, desks, and work surfaces are without splinters.
____ Elevator runs smoothly up/down (semiannual inspection).

Explain any deficiencies noted above:

_____

ENVIRONMENTAL

____ Indoor air quality is not a cause of complaints.
____ Noise levels are not excessive or cause complaints.
____ Temperatures are not too high or low, fluctuate, or are unable to control.
____ Vibrations are not evident.
____ Illumination is not too bright, too dim, or unable to adjust.
____ Ventilation is proper to control temperature and odors.

Explain any deficiencies noted above:

_____

TOOLS (MAINLY FACILITIES)

____ Electrical tools have cords that are not frayed/cut; ground plugs are not missing.
____ Wooden-handled tools are free of splinters and broken shafts.
____ Metal tools are not bent, and chisels are sharp.
____ All tools are stored in appropriate boxes, cabinets, and are not left lying around.

Explain any deficiencies noted above:

_____

ELECTRICAL

___ Switches/outlets are not cracked/broken, and they have secure covers.

___ Extension cords are free of frayed ends and cuts, and they are kept out of walkways.

___ Circuit breaker panels are easily accessible.

___ All circuit breakers are clearly marked as to what they turn off and on.

___ All cords of any type are kept out of walkways to prevent tripping.

Explain any deficiencies noted above:

_____

VEHICLES

___ Vehicles are kept clean, and materials inside them are stored away from the driver.

___ Safety equipment is in good order (wiper, turn signals, horn, seat belts, emergency kits in trunk, and so on).

___ Tires, windshield, and brakes are in good condition.

Explain any deficiencies noted above:

_____

MACHINES AND EQUIPMENT

___ Copy machines and microfiche readers are in good condition.

___ Any microwaves, refrigerators, and coffee makers are in good condition.

___ Printers are in good condition.

___ Computers are in good condition.

___ Electrically powered desk equipment (adding machines, pencil sharpener) are in good condition.

Explain any deficiencies noted above:

_____

CHEMICALS, FUELS, AND LUBRICANTS

___ Chemicals and fuel are stored in fireproof cabinets.

___ Protective equipment is available as required by SDS (MSDS).

____ Warning signs and labels are posted on cabinets where chemicals are stored.
____ SDS are readily available for immediate use.
____ Gasoline and diesel are stored/marked in an approved container.

Explain any deficiencies noted above:

_____

For more information about chemical communication safety, reference https://www.osha.gov/Publications/HazComm_QuickCard_SafetyData.html.

MISCELLANEOUS

____ Ladders, extension, and step type are in good shape, not bent or broken.
____ Bulletin boards are accessible, safety minutes are posted, and OSHA poster is posted.
____ Carts to move books are in good shape, free from rough edges, and casters are okay.

Explain any deficiencies noted above:

_____

SIGNATURES OF EMPLOYEES CONDUCTING INSPECTION:

_____

_____

Date inspection reviewed by Safety Committee: _____

Date inspection reviewed by Administrator: _____

Action taken to correct deficiencies noted and by whom:

_____

_____

_____

_____

_____

_____

APPENDIX G
Contingency Planning for Natural Disasters

The following checklists offer librarians questions to ask in order to identify, quantify, control, and mitigate the risks of natural disasters.

FLOOD PLANNING

    a. What are likely sources of floodwaters, heavy rainfall, snow melt, or hurricane?

    b. How will water enter buildings? Through windows and doors? Through plumbing systems? Gradual seepage?

    c. What is the maximum water level expected?

    d. How wide of an area will be affected by flooding?

    e. Will the library become surrounded by water and inaccessible to emergency help?

    f. Could floodwater close down essential transportation routes?

EARTHQUAKE PLANNING

    a. Are shelving units secured to each other and to the walls?

    b. Are heavy items such as floor copiers and printers secured to avoid sliding or other movement?

    c. Are windows coated to avoid shattering?

    d. Are doors left open after an earthquake warning to allow for escape?

    e. Are hanging lights provided with extra hanging space to allow for swing and to avoid breakage of units?

    f. Is there an emergency shutoff for gas lines and water lines to use after an earthquake warning?

    g. Is there an evacuation plan, and is it understood by the staff? Is there regular review of evacuation plans and practice drills?

    h. Are there posted signs for the public regarding action needed on their part for their protection?

    i. For older buildings, are there plans for retrofitting to improve earthquake stability?

    j. Is the possibility of an earthquake included in new construction planning?

WINTER HAZARDS PLANNING

a. What equipment needs protection from freeze-ups?
b. Is heating equipment capable of maintaining building temperatures above forty degrees?
c. Are any facilities (such as book storage facilities) unoccupied? Does security check these facilities on weekends and nights?
d. Are alternative fuel equipment and supplies maintained so they will be operational in an emergency?
e. Are portable heaters and emergency equipment available?
f. Are snow loads on building roofs checked? Is drainage adequate for melting snow?
g. Will snow or ice prohibit access to the building?

WINDSTORM PLANNING

a. Are critical areas of the library identified?
b. Are proper shutdown procedures for vital equipment known?
c. Are back-up communications (cell phones, two-way radios), phone numbers, and contacts available?
d. Is an off-site emergency center available outside of the windstorm area?
e. Are vital records protected or can they be relocated?
f. Do you maintain ongoing agreements with contractors for supplies and repair work?
g. Do you inspect and repair the roof covering prior to windstorm season?
h. Do you provide shutters or plywood for window protection?
i. Are storm surge or flooding potentials identified and emergency equipment available to remove water?

APPENDIX H

Sample Request for Proposal—Insurance Brokerage Services

PROPERTY AND CASUALTY LINES OF COVERAGE

Section I. Introduction and General Information

A. The [*insert library name*] (hereafter referred to as the Library) is seeking proposals from qualified firms to provide a full range of brokerage and risk management services, including marketing and placement of insurance coverage and consulting on coverage issues and self-insurance operations. One or more firms will be selected to fulfill these needs. (If there is an incumbent broker insert information when the current brokerage contract is set to expire.)

B. The successful respondents will be required to enter into a five-year contract commencing [*insert date*]. The Library reserves the right to cancel the contract at the end of each annual period by giving at least 60 days' prior written notice, or to cancel with cause at any time giving 60 days' notice.

C. To assist firms in preparing their proposals, general background information on the Library is provided in Section II of this request. For additional information, contact [*insert contact information*].

D. Scope: This Request for Proposal contains instructions governing the proposals to be submitted and the material to be included therein, mandatory requirements that must be met to be eligible for consideration, and other requirements to be met by each proposal.

E. All proposals must be received no later than [*insert date*] at the office of XXXXXX

XXXXXX copies of each proposal shall be provided. Copies provided on a CD/USB/other digital storage device are acceptable provided digital copies are provided in PDF [*insert format required*].

Proposals must be sent by mail, or courier, or delivered by person. Under no circumstance will a telephone or fax or e-mailed bid be accepted. Failure of the postal service or a courier, overnight express, or similar service to deliver the proposal package on time shall not be grounds to consider a late bid.

F. The Library reserves the right to waive formalities and reject any and all proposals.

Section II. Background Information

A. [*Insert background information about the Library here. For example, "Library XXXXXX has the largest collection of feminist literature."*]

B. The Library's property and casualty risk and insurance management program is administered by
XXXXXX [*insert name of person at the library responsible for the program*].

C. The Library has XXXXX locations, with total insurable values of $XXXXX. Library collections include
XXXXX # of books, valued at $XXXXX
XXXXX # of media valued at $XXXXX [*Include description: examples may include CDs, microfilms, electronic media, kindle, e- books.*]

D. The Library currently has XXXXX full-time employees and an annual payroll of $XXXXX.

E. The Library currently owns and operates a fleet of approximately XXXXX vehicles.

Section III. Performance Requirements
The successful brokers shall

- provide broker services for the Library in accordance with the requirements and provisions stated herein;
- seek competitive programs and market lines of coverage on an unbiased basis and in the best interests of the Library;
- conduct annual stewardship meetings and reviews that summarize activities and placements on behalf of the Library, including fees and commissions, and future plans;
- prepare an annual market analysis and forecast by insurance line. This summary will include information on trends, market availability, pricing, and long-term market directions;
- assist the Library in the design of policy forms and programs as needed;
- verify the accuracy and adequacy of all binders, policies, policy endorsements, invoices, and other insurance-related documents;
- issue certificates of insurance and answer coverage questions;
- assist in the preparation of underwriting data, statements of values, specifications, and other data required by insurers;
- assist the Library in preparation of proofs of loss or claims reports, and in obtaining loss settlements from insurers;
- attend meetings as requested; and
- be fully qualified and competent with the proper license, knowledge, experience, and personnel.

Evaluation and Award Process
A. The Library shall use its best judgment in conducting a comparative assessment of the proposals.

B. The Library shall select finalists that appear to have the ability to service the Library's needs. The Library is not bound to accept the lowest-priced proposal if that proposal is not in the best interests of the library as determined by the Library in its sole discretion. The Library will use the following criteria (in no particular order):

- Market expertise and access to insurers
- Demonstrated ability to identify emerging issues for consideration, and ways to assist the Library in dealing with those concerns
- Demonstrated insight and understanding of library risk management and insurance operations and markets
- Demonstrated ability to evaluate and make recommendations concerning appropriate risk retention levels and alternatives available to the Library
- Extent and type of services provided
- Qualifications and experience of the assigned account executive, team, and personnel
- Explanation of the services, programs, and products that the Broker provides to assist and support risk management at the Library
- References that the Library may contact, especially in the library sector
- Cost of proposal

RFP Cancellation

The Library reserves the right to cancel this Request for Proposal at any time prior to award, without penalty.

Insurance

Once awarded, the Contractor shall maintain insurance at all times during the performance of this brokerage services contract. The Contractor represents that at time of acceptance of any contract, that the Contractor maintains comprehensive general liability insurance in the amount of not less than $1,000,000 combined single limit, workers' compensation insurance as required by law, and automobile liability insurance for all vehicles used by the Contractor in performance of the specified work. The Contractor must maintain professional liability (errors and omissions) in an amount of not less than $1,000,000 per occurrence, $2,000,000 per aggregate. Upon request, the Contractor shall provide proof of such coverages.

Section IV. Services Required and Specifications
A. Risk Identification and Evaluation

With the assistance of Library employees, broker will review operations of the Library for potential for material loss of financial resources as a result of either direct or indirect consequences, develop and evaluate all necessary information required to assess material exposures, and educate and inform the Library and underwriters for potential loss.

Mandatory services in this category, required to be included in base fee, include the following services:

- Ongoing risk assessment/exposure analysis
- Analysis of the Library's risk financing options, and risk retention levels to achieve optimal cost benefit to the Library
- Meetings with Library officials, and surveys of the Library's operations

B. Insurance Market Submission Preparation and Review

Mandatory services in this category, required to be included in the basic fee, include the following services:

- Knowledge of the capabilities and security of carriers
- Awareness of specialty carriers
- Risk management program design recommendations
- Develop marketing plan timeline
- Prepare program specification and underwriting submissions
- Collect, maintain, and use Library underwriting data
- Prepare annual "state of insurance market" report
- All current insurance placed by current broker (if applicable)

C. Insurance Procurement

Subject to the direction and control of the Library, the Broker will be responsible to conduct all insurance procurement of all current insurance (if applicable) and any other additional insurance program, which may be appropriate to finance the Library's risk.

Mandatory services in this category, required to be included in the base fee, include the following services:

- Monitor insurance marketplace and keep the Library informed of any significant changes or trends. Provide forecast of insurance market conditions prior to annual renewals.
- Analyze market pricing and make recommendations.
- Conduct negotiations with insurance markets.
- Submit summary of quotes to the designated personnel at the Library for selection of coverage and insurer.
- Provide analysis and comparison of program alternatives and pricing.
- Explain coverage and wording changes in any policies at renewal.
- Place coverage at the direction of the Library.

D. Program Administration and Execution

Mandatory services in this category, required to be included in the base fee, include the following services:

- Provide coverage summaries and binders prior to the date of policy expiration.
- Review and provide timely and accurate policies and endorsements.
- Answer coverage questions.
- Issue certificates of insurance, auto identification cards, and other program documents as required.
- Review premium audits, including retrospective rating adjustments.
- Attend meetings with Library personnel to discuss risk management programs.
- Provide consultation services with respect to coverage and how it is applied to various Library business activities and events.
- Be available during regular business hours to answer questions about the Library's coverage, and other risk management issues.
- Monitor carriers' financial information and alert the Library when a carrier's standards fall below acceptable requirements.
- Full disclosure of all compensation with respect to insurance premiums.

E. Claims Services

The Library will prepare and sign a letter of authority allowing the selected firm to operate as the library's claims advocate on all policies issued prior to the effective date of the resultant Broker Services Contract.

Mandatory services in this category, required to be included in the base fee, include the following services:

- Liaison with carriers, serving as an advocate for the Library.
- Follow all claims assigned to conclusion.
- Periodic claims review.
- Provide assistance with proof of loss and other claims documentation.
- Assist in the resolution of coverage issues, including coverage interpretation, disputes, reservation of rights letters, etc.
- Coordinate claims reporting to primary and/or excess underwriters.

Section V. Information Required from Respondents

1. Cover letter
2. Qualifications—resumes of key individuals
3. Professional references (provide minimum number)
4. Describe and explain how you plan to provide mandatory services listed in the prior section. Describe and explain optional services.

5. Cost of proposal—provide an itemized list; please describe those services included in the annual fee and those services that are not.
6. Provide a certificate of insurance.
7. Please provide any additional information or data not requested as part of this RFP that you believe should be considered in the evaluation of a response.
8. Describe any additional services that you believe could have any significant benefit to the Library.
9. Describe any other considerations that you believe are important to the design, implementation, and analysis of the Library's insurance program.

About the Authors

Sally Alexander serves as director of risk management and chief risk officer for Colorado State University (CSU). She manages the operations of the Office of Risk Management and Insurance (RMI) and leads institutional risk management efforts on campus. She served on the board of directors of the University Risk Management and Insurance Association (URMIA) from 2013 to 2017 and co-chaired URMIA's Governmental Regulatory Affairs Committee during that same period. She has co-presented at various URMIA conferences and sessions. In 2019 she was awarded CSU's Office of International Programs' Distinguished Service Award in recognition of outstanding contributions to the internationalization of CSU. Prior to joining CSU in 2008 she worked for Larimer County as a risk manager. Originally from South Africa, she practiced law in the field of insurance law. She has a BA degree from the University of Witwatersrand, Johannesburg, South Africa; an LLB (bachelor of laws) degree from Rhodes University, Grahamstown, South Africa; and a master's degree in environmental policy and management from the University of Denver, Colorado. She also has an associate's degree in risk management and a master's of business administration from CSU.

Mary Breighner is a chartered property and casualty underwriter (CPCU). She was formerly the vice president and global practice leader for FM Global, where she oversaw and guided the accounts and account servicing of more than 300 colleges and universities, as well as hundreds of public schools, governmental entities, and hospitals worldwide. She remains an active member of the University Risk Management and Insurance Association (URMIA) and has served on various committees there, as an officer, director, and past president. She received the Distinguished Risk Manager Award from URMIA in 1992. In 2003 she became an affiliate member of URMIA's board of directors. Breighner holds the CPCU designation. She has presented nationally and internationally on higher education and public entity risk management and insurance issues at numerous national and regional conferences. She coauthored the 2005 edition of this book and has published numerous articles in *URMIA Journal*.

Jeanne M. Drewes was chief of the Binding and Collections Care Section of the Preservation Directorate at the Library of Congress from 2006 to 2019 and is currently a cultural heritage consultant. Formerly, she was assistant director for access and preservation at Michigan State University Libraries and was head of the Preservation Department of the Milton S. Eisenhower Library at Johns Hopkins University. Drewes received the Ross Atkinson Lifetime Achievement Award in 2017. She received her MALS degree from the University of Missouri–Columbia and was a Mellon Intern for Preservation Administration at the University of Michigan. She is an active member of ALA, the American Institute for Conservation, the International Federation of Library Associations and Institutions, and the Guild of Bookworkers. For forty years, Drewes has taught workshops and published on the topics of insurance and risk management, disaster planning, preservation outreach, and other areas of preservation. She was the managing editor for the 2005 edition of this book.

Index

schedule policies, 88
security. *See* loss prevention; safety
self-insurance, 7, 73–74
self-insured retention (SIR) clauses, 73,
    110, 127
shootings, 59–60
slips and falls, 65, 126
smoking, policies against, 51
social engineering fraud, 61–62, 101
sovereign immunity, 62–63
special collections, 37–38, 46, 60–61,
    97–98, 121–122, 143
special events, risk from, 25
sprinkler systems, 48–52, 146
staff. *See* employees
statement of values (SOV), 87
storms, 53, 54, 152
strategic planning, 12, 14–16
strategy settings, 10, 12
structures. *See* buildings
subrogation, 72, 85, 104
surety bonds, 115–116

T

terrorism coverage, 93, 111
theft, 60–61, 100. *See also* fraud
time-element coverage, 98–99
torts, 23, 39–41, 101
transfer of risk, 7, 71–73
transit, property in, 92, 95
trustees, 1–2, 12, 23, 108–109,
    139–140

U

umbrella liability coverage, 106–107
U.S. Government Publishing Office (GPO),
    37

V

valuable papers, 20, 38, 59, 97–98,
    121–122
valuation
    actual cash value *vs.* replacement
        cost, 28, 95–96
    of books and materials, 32–39, 96–98
    of personal property, 30–32
    of real property, 28–30
    resources for, 136–137
vandalism, 59
vehicles. *See* automobiles
volunteers, liability of, 111–112

W

waivers, 63, 72
water damage, 59, 121–122. *See also* floods
water sprinkler systems, 48–52, 146
weather and natural disasters, 52–57, 93,
    151–152
wet pipe systems, 49
windstorms, 53, 152
winter hazards, 54, 152
workers' compensation, 63–65, 72,
    107–108, 111, 124
workplace harassment, 68
worst-case scenarios, 41